M000115442

FIRE YOUR JOB
HIRE
YOUR
PASSION

Billy F. Wroe Jr.

Foreword by Taralyn Michelle

Purpose Publishing
1503 Main Street #168
Grandview, Missouri 64030
www.PurposePublishing.com

Fire Your Job, Hire Your Passion
Copyright © 2022 by 1stWroe LLC
ISBN: 978-1-0879-0865-6

All rights reserved. No part of this publication may be reproduced, distributed, or transmitted in any form or by any means, including photocopying, recording, or other electronic or mechanical methods, without the prior written permission of the publisher, except in the case of brief quotations embodied in critical reviews and certain other noncommercial uses permitted by copyright law. Printed in the United States of America.

www.1stWroe.com

Contents

Foreword

The journey. We all have one we're on. It takes time to see the pattern and find our stride. Our divine design eventually connects with divine timing and leads to living out our divine assignment. Sometimes we're so focused on the intricacies of our journey that we miss the significance of the point of intersection with someone else's. However, I remember the exact point of intersection with Billy F. Wroe Jr. I was a host on a radio show back in the day and on this particular episode we were discussing relationships. Live shows are interesting. You never know what you're going to get and for me that was part of the thrill. At this point in the conversation, remarks had been surface and crowd pleasing with clear sides established. Then, the next caller came through the cue.

This caller had a perspective that was neutral enough to invite others into the conversation yet refined enough to make his position clear. Communicating objectively is an acquired skill that requires removing your personal experiences and emotion. This caller genuinely wanted to understand others while encouraging deeper thought; not asserting his opinion. He wasn't about being the end-all-be-all. He wasn't interested in claiming a side. Instead, he approached the conversation with a curiosity and intellect that acted as fresh water washing away the smell of urine in the air from the pissing contest.

Billy Wroe was on the scene, and he instantly became an audience and network favorite. I looked forward to his perspective and eventually we began chatting about any and everything off air. When I was introduced to Billy's company 1stWroe, it all made sense. "You always want to be on the first row because the people on the first row have nothing between them and information being presented." This was the reason why Billy's way of communicating naturally included and never excluded others. Whether you agree or disagree with him you never felt like what you wanted to share wasn't welcomed or valued.

Beyond his intellect and openness was a wisdom that came from navigating his share of life experiences that I sensed were impactful. Yet, for years we never had those conversations. Sure, we shared like friends do when we chatted: spouses, children, work, goals and just about anything else. Still, I sensed there was a space that remained closed. We had a conversation once where Billy shared with me how he learned how to write and not make the story about him. This was an interesting share because I felt like I knew of him without really knowing him in our friendship at that time. This would soon change.

In 2019 I published my first book entitled *The Ultimate Release* and was nervously excited to share this new development with my brilliant friend. As always Billy was there to support as he is with all of his friends. I appreciated his feedback, but I felt like feedback and support for those privileged enough to know him wasn't enough. By this time, I'd learned a little more about my friend and what became clear was his divine design was calling. His expression of his experiences mattered, and they matter right now.

Heeding the Call

Billy and I have a routine. We bounce ideas off one another and strategize on how to manifest what we desire. We coach each other and challenge each other accordingly. Billy would share the most amazing projects he was working on like, one of my favorites, his relationship calculator. Who comes up with a scale of probability based on certain characteristics that is ridiculously accurate?

There's all of this anointing concentrated in this confined space that was shared sparingly with a select few. This was not what Billy was created to do or who he was designed to be. So, on this day it was his turn to be called to the carpet. I nudged gently on and off throughout the years, "Billy, you have to share your wisdom with others. People need to have your perspective as an option. It's your gift and not meant to be kept." He always said he would, and he tried, but life.

Finally, the moment had come. I needed him to move because now was the time. I could feel it. I launched my company Divine Design Media LLC and part of what I do for a living is help people navigate their life story then support them in sharing those stories with the world. My gift is being able to see God's gifts in others then connecting with them spiritually to support them in stepping into who they were created to be.

He was ready even if he wasn't sure. And I wasn't sure whether he was sure or not. All I knew was I couldn't take no for an answer. I believe we intersected for this moment in time. So, I spoke Billy's language. I proposed a challenge. "Billy, if you start your book now, your manuscript can be finished by December 31st of 2021. I'll be with you every step of the way as your accountability partner. I believe in you and your gift. This book is more than a book. It's the beginning of you accepting your divine design and beginning your divine assignment. I've listened to you talk about this and now is your time to be about it and change countless lives including your own. This is the beginning of what you know you're meant to do. So, you in?" Billy's response? "Let me pull up my calendar." That conversation took place in late February 2021.

Divine Timing

I received chapter one from Billy on March 8th, and chapters two and three on March 21st. April through June brought forth chapters four, five, and six while chapters seven through thirteen were completed between July 25th through October 24th. By November the publishing company had the completed manuscript for *Fire Your Job, Hire Your Passion*. As I read through the chapters it was a whole experience. I couldn't stop. From the bar in several airports and in-flight, in Uber's, at home, and even when being annoyed when interrupted by clients. I thought this book was about leaving Corporate America and pursuing your passion. Instead, the core of this book speaks to the human condition of navigating the complexities of skewed identity and wavering belief.

Passion is an extension of our divine design in that your divine assignment is your passion. But what happens when you're unclear about *why*; *why* you are? What warmed my heart the most as I read were the prompts demonstrating what to fire to lose dead weight and what to hire to become clear on your *why*. There is a multifaceted clarity on the *why* that leads to *who,* then supports how to *be* in life. I believe this will get the reader closer to discovering their divine design and assignment. The gift that keeps on giving are the breadcrumbs leading readers to divine timing and alignment like the flow Billy experienced in every aspect of his life once he started writing. *Fire Your Job, Hire Your Passion* serves as a blueprint to do just that.

In chapter eight, *Adjusting Your Frequency - Giving Notice,* Billy discusses the two-way signal; what we receive from others as well as what we're broadcasting to others. How fitting. I consider it a blessing to receive his signal and the manuscript was confirmation. I was surprised to learn of his fears and insecurities. But then, being created for service myself, I shouldn't have been. We were created to support and instinctively that's what we do first. However, accepting the invitation to take on our higher self makes blurred spots clear.

Fire Your Job, Hire Your Passion is true to Billy F. Wroe Jr.; a soul divinely created to give of himself in the hope that others will either find their *why* or connect deeper to it. *Who* we were uniquely created to be depends on it. Indeed, we all have a journey and now you have a valuable tool to access along yours. Happy reading.

Taralyn Michelle
CEO Divine Design Media LLC
www.TaralynMichelle.com

A Required Prescription
(About the Book)

When we typically meet a person for the first time in a social setting, at some point in the conversation, the person will probably ask us the classic "Getting-to-know-you" question... "What do you do?" So often, I have answered this question with the title of my current 9 - 5. As a result, I have been a Retail Representative, Customer Service Agent, Network Marketer, and many other labels during these conversations. But what if I told you that we are confusing the question? What people subconsciously are looking for us to answer is, "What are we passionate about?" What pushes us through the days that we don't want to go to the place where we simply "Earn a living"? The answer to that question and the excitement that it arouses is much more potent than an Analyst, Software Designer, or CEO will ever be.

Part of the problem is that we are conditioned not to answer the question correctly. Instead, we use our profession as a haven to keep from humiliating ourselves. Also, many of us are entirely ignorant that we want to be asked the more important question. Why? Because a more meaningful response further invests us into our interdependent experience within humanity. See, we do so much more than the titles that enable us to provide for ourselves and our loved ones. Still, for some reason, many of us spend our entire lives focused on placing our careers in the limelight while missing multiple opportunities to lead with our passion during our initial introduction.

As a person who has spent a significant amount of my time reflecting on, researching, and experimenting with growth and inspiration, I have had more than my fair share of conversations with friends, acquaintances, co-workers, mentors, and even strangers on the topic of passion. In many of those passion-driven conversations, I am asked 1 of 2 questions. Either "How do you find your passion?" or "How do you know when you find what you are passionate about?" *Fire Your Job, Hire Your Passion* aims to answer these questions in a manner that resonates with common-sense solutions and makes the daily application process easy to implement. I sincerely hope that by the end of this book, you experience a paradigm shift that moves your Passion into a pole position ahead of your Job.

I will provide you with a prescription to prepare you for this book's simple yet powerful concepts. This prescription will not be something that you take to your local pharmacy to have filled. Instead, this will be the first seed of decision-making that I'd like to ask you to nurture as we journey through this book together. The prescription is this: If you are who you are today because of whom you practiced being yesterday, who are you practicing to be for tomorrow? Is that who you want to be? I have lived by this mantra for the past six years, and the results driven by keeping this mindset at the forefront of my decision making have been phenomenal. Rather than allowing circumstance and chance to dictate today's rendition of Billy Wroe, I am intentionally practicing in each moment for the next, based on who I authentically desire to be. Now that does not mean that there are not days that I miss my mark, but the next day, even the next moment, is an opportunity to begin practicing for a better result.

Fire Your Job, Hire Your Passion is not about literally firing your job. At no point during this book will I ask you to walk into your boss's office to submit your resignation or quit. Though this is the path that I ultimately chose for myself, I realized that I fired my job years before I actually walked out of the door. This is also not a book designed to permit ourselves to begin producing subpar results at work. If it were, the title would be *Get Fired from Your Job, Hope to Get Hired by Your Passion*. At all times, the goal is to be patient with our growth process while remaining in continual pursuit of both our personal and professional excellence. Understand that this is more about adopting a mindset that drives purposeful actions rather than get-rich-quick behaviors.

The book will require us to be both vulnerable and brutally honest as we answer some difficult questions about who we want to be and plot a course on how to align those desires using the raw materials of the person we are in that very moment. Throughout the book, you will encounter what I refer to as **Passion Points** and **Timeouts**. Passion Points are little nuggets designed to help stimulate internal dialogue. Oftentimes we know the question, but we refuse to ask it. The purpose of Passion Points is to do just that. Timeouts are designed to create immediate breaks in your reading in order to shift the focus back to you. They are best described as small impromptu exercises that you can mentally workout with as often as you'd like until your results are what you desire them to be based upon a collaborative combination of your thoughts, actions, and emotions.

Whether we comprehend it or not, our passion is woven into our legacy. We can either leave behind a powerful echo that resounds throughout generations or a faint memory that fades into the background within the lifetime of our peers. The choice is ours to make. If you proceed beyond this point, I ask that you commit to seeing *Fire Your Job, Hire Your Passion* all the way through to the end. At times it will feel unbearably uncomfortable, and you may even have moments when you want to give up, but always remember that the person who comes out on the other side of adversity is never the same as the one who went into it. With that said, I will ask you the same question that I ask my oldest son during our conversations about challenging growth. Are you willing to do the work? If the answer is Yes, then let's get started! Allow me to welcome you to *Fire Your Job, Hire Your Passion*!

THE LAYOFFS
(Eliminating Roadblocks)

CHAPTER 1

You Have a Job to Do

I t was the end of a typical workday in my office. As per usual, I packed my laptop, gathered my things, and said my goodbyes for the evening. The last goodbye as I headed for the door was always to my boss, but this day, as I said goodbye, he looked at his watch and made a passive-aggressive comment that stopped me in my tracks. "You can't come in after me and leave before me." Though it was said in a jovial tone, as with all comedy, there was some truth of observation mixed in with it. At that moment I had to make a choice. I could either laugh off the comment and continue home, or I could stop and address what was really on my mind. I chose to stop.

Once I assured my boss that all work tasks for the day had been completed, I made a statement that most people who want to remain employed would probably keep to themselves. I told him that rather than being concerned about when I was leaving work (on time), the more pressing area of concern was that as of late I had been struggling to find the motivation to even come into work at all. In the midst of all the challenges that were taking place for me personally, I was now approaching the professional crossroads between making money in an unhealthy environment or improving my own mental health so that I could pursue my passion. As a "Responsible" adult I always thought that I would be obligated to choose the money. However, the more I wrestled with how much irreplaceable time the money was costing me, the easier the choice to pursue my passion became. Let's see what those numbers actually look like.

According to the Bureau of Labor Statistics, in 2018, the average full-time employed American 25 years and older worked about 8.50 hours per day (5 days a week). That means that on average, 42.5 of our 168 hours in a week (25.3%) are spent in front of computers, on production lines, delivering goods, in meetings, and unfortunately for many of us, away from our passions. Once we begin to factor in additional activities such as sleep, eating, social media, commuting, and grooming, we find ourselves with less than 65 hours (40%) remaining in our entire week to do everything else. In many cases, a lot of the available time is used to recover from the prior work week before the next one begins. The disheartening part about these statistics is that many people are either working well beyond 65 years of age or finding themselves back at work due to inadequate retirement planning and increases in their living costs.

Whether you are an employee, self-employed, business owner, investor, or on welfare, we all require some income source to survive in this capitalist era. To maintain the flow of that income requires some form of effort on our parts. For employees and business owners, the effort is easy to see on the surface as they trade time for money. Investors' efforts are a little more inconspicuous, as they allow their money to work in the background. Welfare seems as if there is no effort required at all, but though you may not see it, I can tell you based on my personal experience, even people on welfare have a job to do.

When I was 23 years old, I became a single father, suffered from major depression, and lost my job in the same year. As a result, I went on welfare to help bridge my unemployment gap. None of the aid that I received came simply because I was experiencing unfortunate, and in many ways, self-inflicted circumstances. After going through the application process, I was awarded about $550 a month in cash aid and $460 in food stamps. As a result of my drastic change in income, I also had to move out of my house, I allowed my car to be repossessed, and fortunately, I moved in with my sister who gave me a room at her place to share with my 2-year-old son. Imagine how that drop from a fairly independent young man to the verge of homelessness awakens the senses. To survive, I had to reduce my lifestyle significantly.

I remember about a year into my welfare experience; I was sitting in a meeting with my social worker. She explained some of the additional benefits available to me for daycare and school. In that same conversation, she also explained how I would have to remain "qualified" for welfare. I would only be able to make so much money before losing my benefits, so rushing out to find a full-time job that pays too much should not be a goal. Also, getting married could potentially disqualify me due to a jump in my household income. From the beginning, I knew that welfare was only temporary for me, but at that moment, I committed to making it the shortest possible leg of my journey. It was important for me to rediscover the financial trajectory I was on before my depression. I understood that remaining financially dependent upon a system that limited my financial independence was not a compatible foundation for building my new lifestyle.

Our financial stability is important, but how we define that stability and at what cost is equally important. Back when the Baby Boomers entered the workforce, finding stable opportunities and understanding the cost was more simplistic. Many Boomers would find a company to work for 40 years and then retire with a pension. I call this the 1 x 40 retirement formula. Though it may sound like a sweet deal on the surface, remember that on average, 60% of our time is spent at work, sleeping, eating, commuting, and grooming. That means that barring any illness, out of 4 decades of your life, you have about 15 years to do what you want to do. The 1 x 40 retirement formula is almost all but forgotten in today's workplace. Today's retirement formula is more convoluted, with such variables as layoffs, entrepreneurship, unemployment, student loans, company extinction-level events, outsourcing, artificial intelligence, machine learning, and other new technologies. In addition to the added complexity within the workspace, social media has hyper imposed the desire to accumulate possessions that help us appear successful to our peers, causing many people to take on unhealthy levels of debt. With these conditions, it can almost feel impossible to live within our means to achieve retirement, let alone make space for our passion.

Living Beyond Your Means

A small single-page comic that I came across many years ago really spoke to me about our almost instinctual desire to accumulate more stuff. In the first panel, the comic showed a person in a sports car looking up at a person in a helicopter, wishing that they too owned a helicopter. The second panel showed a guy in a standard car wishing he had the sports car. The third panel showed a person walking, wishing he had the standard car. Finally, the fourth panel showed a person without shoes, simply wishing that he had shoes. In each panel, the person was so caught up looking at what someone else had that they did not appreciate what they themselves had that others were still striving to obtain. This type of behavior prompts many Americans to live on 100% of their net income, or even worse, over 100% of it. As a result, living beyond our means will be the first job mentality that we call into the office to fire.

A good friend of mine once told me that money is power because it provides influence. I always considered that influence to be external. Still, as I explored in-depth the behaviors that pull us away from our passions, I realized that money also has internal governance over our decisions. There is something liberating about having the ability to pay your own way. Thus, it is not a coincidence that shortly after we start our first job, we acquire our first bill. As we embark on our journey towards independence, we must inevitably use the resources we acquire along the way. Whether or not we use those resources efficiently is another story. Living beyond our means is an effortless discipline that occurs because most of us develop our spending habits at an unmoderated pace. We wait years before reassessing those habits, if we ever reassess them at all. I remember when I got my first credit card at 17 years of age. As a result, I quickly accumulated $750 of entertainment, junk food, and electronic device debt before turning 18. As a 17-year-old, you do not need to have a plan on how to spend $750. Believe me, it comes naturally. Within a few short weeks, on top of the $700 a month that I earned working part-time at $7 per hour, I spent over a months-worth of wages in credit card debt. The trap had been set. I was now locked into my job, and my ability to earn money was no longer a choice of convenience. In short, the effortless discipline I initially took for granted now required effort to maintain. This scenario is not far off from the life of many adults today.

Based on data from Nerdwallet, as of June 2019, the average American household carried on average $6,829 in revolving credit card debt, while a 2018 study by Magnify Money showed that the median savings account balance was $4,830. Magnify Money also reported that almost 1 out of 3 American households had a savings account balance of $0. So the average household has a net worth of -$1,999, and 1 out of 3 have a net worth of -$6,829. These situations combined are recipes for financial disaster and signal that people are no longer just living from paycheck-to-paycheck; rather, some have fallen behind by 1 to 2 paychecks altogether. When we choose to live in this type of financial space, we create enormous mental pressure for our jobs to be the top priority over all things. As adults, our bills like rent, food, transportation, and clothing even more so lock us into our jobs. We cannot afford to miss a single paycheck, and as a result, we begin to sacrifice family, health, and even quality of life, as our passions slip further down on the things-to-do list. Here is where our common sense must partner with our habits to create a solution that corrects this imbalance. Living beyond our means, we are going to have to let you go.

Timeout: Net Worth

*Grab your **Passion Journal**. Take a moment to ask yourself the following 2 questions. You may need to do some research to determine your answers.*

- *Is your net worth positive or negative?*
  - * **Net worth**: Value of all of your Assets minus all of your Debts.*
- *Can you afford to take 2 weeks off unpaid and dedicate that time to invest in something you are passionate about?*

Living within our means does not mean that we cannot strive for greater things financially in life. It does not even mean that the life we live presently has to be subpar. Living within our means is simply before we reach out to grasp immediate or distant financial goals, we intentionally move within closer proximity of the goal to make it easier to obtain and maintain. This is accomplished by shifting our reward system disciplines away from an instant gratification model into delayed gratification.

Urgency Calibration

Let's say that you want to go out to dinner at an expensive restaurant. You have the choice between going the first week in the month and being broke until the end of the month, or you could pack a lunch for the next 2 weeks and afford the same dinner with the money you have saved. The challenge in this type of scenario is that most people habitually choose instant gratification. We tell ourselves that we have a taste for something and jump into action to fulfill that desire. We also tell ourselves that we are disciplined enough to go to dinner the first week and pack our lunch for the following 2 weeks when we have not packed lunch in the last 12 months. To arrive at a place where we can begin to contemplate the benefits of delayed gratification, our sense of urgency must be properly calibrated so that we can create an intentional pause in all of our non-urgent decision making. For myself, I have found that the 2 most effective methods of calibrating a sense of urgency have come in the forms of issue identification and by embracing proactive approaches. To understand the first method, issue identification, let's put on our science hats for a moment.

Issue Identification

When it comes to identifying issues, our brains work similarly to that of an orchestra. There are times when every section will play simultaneously, moments of silence, and everything in between. The two main "instrument sections" in the brain that help with issue identification are memory and logic. Memory acts as our own personal live camera crew. As we perform our day-to-day lives, a crescendo of activity fires in the areas of our brain responsible for memory. Depending upon whether we are experiencing an auditory sensation, emotional response, physical touch, geographical location, or another memory-triggering event, we will store the corresponding information differently. Located in the frontal lobe of the brain is the prefrontal cortex. The prefrontal cortex manages many of our logical processes and works to analyze, organize, and surmise our perceived relationship between cause and effect. When partnered together, our memory and logic's power help us develop what is known as familiarity. Just as with our physical environment, the more familiar we are with our surroundings, the easier it is for us to navigate within it. The same holds true for issue identification. The more familiar we are with an issue, the easier it becomes to identify and navigate.

Think back to when you first mastered the alphabet. Now, think about the first time you saw "X" as a multiplication symbol. Before multiplication was introduced, "X" was simply a letter in the alphabet. You had to become familiar with "X" as a mathematical symbol to know how to identify multiplication problems. Jump a couple of years ahead to algebra, the "X" becomes a variable, and the multiplication symbol is replaced with an asterisk. The multiplication process never changes; however, each symbol change requires you to become familiar with how to identify the problem to properly arrive at a solution. The good news is that this relationship between memory and logic is not static or isolated to mathematical problems. It can be developed and over time applied throughout almost every area of our life.

Absent the presence of brain damage, we can actually improve our memory and logical reasoning skills by building strong stories that we can easily correlate to the behaviors we want to retain. For myself, living within my means was something that I "Said" was important to me, but identifying the issues that kept me from moving from empty words to proper actions was difficult. I had to ask myself, was I really saying what I wanted? Did I really want to live within my means? Surprisingly, the answers to both of those questions were no. I wanted to live an extravagant life filled with travel, adventures, and fun. As a result, I was willing to be broke to accomplish just that. I would spend beyond my excess regularly and devise plans to catch up, only to fall right back behind. Not only was the living-within-my-means story not enough, but it wasn't even true. As a result, a few years ago, I decided to rewrite my story in a manner that resonated better with me and simplified the path to the behaviors that I wanted to practice. The story is concise and starts like many other stories from our childhood...

Once upon a time, there was a man who did not want to work forever. In order to have enough money to make his dream come true, he had to save 25% of all of the money that he earned. Now the man could not afford to save 25% of his income immediately, so he started by saving 12% and committed to adding a minimum of 1% more to the savings percentage each year until he reached his 25% goal.

I realized that our honest desires guide the results of our internal stories, and no matter whether those stories are fiction or nonfiction, they become our truths. How many times have you sat alone with your thoughts while waiting for someone to arrive, allowing yourself to become more and more frustrated or frantic about the reasons for their delayed arrival? By the time they arrive, you have all but convinced yourself about what has happened before they can say a word. As children, how many stories did we create about the monsters in the closet or under our bed? The stories became so significant that we devised ways to protect ourselves from them. My favorite 2 solutions were running and jumping to the bed after turning off the lights in my room and the all-time classic, hiding under the covers. As ridiculous as those solutions may sound to me now, they kept me safe during my childhood.

With my new story on living within my means ingrained, I immediately began saving money like never before. After only 2 years, I was able to save 18% of all of my income. At max, I was only 7 years away from saving 25% of my income a year. The story changed my perspective on saving, which indirectly adjusted my spending habits. For instance, I used to think that my Spotify music subscription was just a $15 bill, no big deal for many people. However, I now find myself asking questions like, do I want to spend money on music that I rarely listen to or add to my savings percentage or travel budget.

- **Passion Point:** What is the "Once upon a time" story that guides your financial discipline?
    - I don't know about investing.
    - I don't make enough money.
    - I can't afford to save.

Whether an instant or delayed gratification decision, issue identification mostly happens in fractions of a second. It is important that we build a strong resonance between our memory and logic to produce the familiarity necessary for improving our overall reaction time between the identification and decision process. By building a stronger and honest story upfront, the behaviors that embody living within our means become easier to see and implement. All that remains to complete the identification process is to ask ourselves the direct question, "Is the issue urgent?" Is that expensive dinner an urgent issue?

Embracing a Proactive Approach

My closest uncle always told me that "You don't have to *get* ready if you *stay* ready." The second step to properly calibrating your sense of urgency is to get ahead of issues proactively. I caution you in advance that the proactive approach is not about using as many preemptive attacks as possible to beat potential situations into submission. Fortunately, I realized this when my oldest son's mother and I separated. To properly calibrate my urgency as his father, I had to prepare myself mentally for the day that he might call another man dad. I did not prepare by finding another woman for him to call mom first (External Preemptive Attack). I simply sat quietly and meditated on some of the emotions that I believed I would feel at that moment. I listened to some of the internal stories I attached to what it meant for him to call another man dad. I explored everything from the ridiculous to the more likely scenarios. Then I asked myself what drove those emotions to lead in the hypothetical experiences. Each one boiled down to my fear of being inadequate as a father and what that meant to my status in manhood (i.e. my ego).

These exercises enabled me to address the primary issue, my insecurities, and establish/reinforce confidence in the fact that I was attempting to be the best father that I could be. By the time Z called someone else dad, I had built up such a strong defense against my own ego that even though I did not like the particular individual, I never once attempted to sway him from the connection. I had already reconciled that just because he referred to another man as a dad did not somehow mean that I was any less his father. More importantly, I found that our son's desire to feel loved by as many people as possible was the top priority, and it would be absurd for me to limit the number of loving men in his life to only me.

- **Passion Point:** How many opportunities have you missed because of a lack of preparation?

There are multiple examples in history where using proactive approaches has paid dividends. When the famous Canadian World War II Fighter Pilot George "Buzz" Beurling was not fighting in dogfights tallying up record numbers in enemy kills, his peers recalled him sitting in the cockpit of his plane going over attack vectors to improve his deflection shooting techniques. As Harriet Tubman led slaves through the underground railroad, she carried a shotgun with her both as a form of protection from the oppressors who wanted to impede her mission and a deterrent to slaves that wanted to turn back due to fear of being caught. Or when Bessie Coleman was denied entry into flight school in the United States, rather than accepting that she could not be a pilot, she taught herself French, moved to France, and became the first African American woman to have a pilot's license. These people did not wait for training to be scheduled **(Buzz)**, until after they encountered adversity **(Harriet)**, or for someone to create laws that were more favorable to their pursuit of happiness **(Bessie)**. Instead, they chose to embrace finding solutions proactively. In my early 20s my peers and I referred to this proactive approach as the 6 P's Principle: Prior Planning Prevents Piss Poor Performance. The more thoughtful our preparation was, the more natural our responses became to the unexpected.

If you were to walk into a class of any martial arts discipline today, within your first conversation, you would hear the words self-defense. Martial arts instructors repeatedly expose their students to real-world scenarios to teach them what actions should be taken if these unexpected circumstances arise. Interestingly enough, how to go out and find conflict is not in the curriculum. Embracing a proactive approach is another powerful tool that can develop an appropriate sense of urgency by helping us become less reactive and more pragmatic in how we resolve unexpected situations. Because in many cases, we are looking at unknown circumstances, the best way I have found to develop this ability is through the use of meditation. Meditation helps us with proactivity by engaging our mind's ability to focus deeply and intentionally on past, present, and future events. Let's start with the unknown future.

Future (Visualization)

What if I told you that we all have access to a time machine in which we can rewind, pause, or even fast forward time? I know it sounds like science fiction, but indulge me for a moment with the following exercise.

Timeout: Traveling to the Future

*Grab your **Passion Journal**. If you need, close your eyes to help immerse yourself in the experience... Grab a single piece of paper. Take a moment to feel the texture of the paper as you hold it in your hands. Now set the paper down and visualize yourself ripping that piece of paper into 4 pieces. Really imagine what that process would be like. Hear the paper's sound as it tears, feel the vibration on your fingertips as you separate each piece, see what each piece looks like after you are done making 4 pieces. Visualize that for about 10 seconds. Now open your eyes and tear the piece of paper into the 4 pieces that you imagined. Write one of the following four words on each piece of paper. "Time Travel Does Exist." Save the 4 pieces of paper in your passion journal or in your book. What just happened?*

If you participated in the exercise, congratulations, you just intentionally used your time machine to briefly travel to the future. A large percentage of the degree of accuracy of that future was dependent upon your action or inaction to tear the paper into 4 pieces. This form of meditation is called visualization, a process where we mentally engage with the steps we intend to make in our minds, prior to physically implementing the actual actions. Now that we have experimented with its application, we are going to set the purpose of the 4 pieces of paper. As you come across information in the book that resonates strongly with you, take 1 piece of paper and use it as a placeholder. Once you have used all 4 and come across another placeholder-worthy concept, you will read the 4 existing placeholders and decide if you want to exchange an old concept for the new one or keep the existing concepts.

Visualization is a critical component of proactive approaches because it helps us to see the future by employing our imagination. Our imaginations delimit us from the boundaries of our present reality. As a result, in theory, there is not a single unknown scenario that we cannot create and eventually solve through its use. Visualization happens on a micro scale for each of us every day before we ever even have to employ our imagination. When we head out the door to a place that we are familiar with, we quickly visualize the destination that we desire and begin to move towards it with very little thought. We do not have to imagine the roads, the parking lot, or the building in order to arrive successfully at our destination. Every week that new movies are released in the box office, we see on a larger scale what can happen when the imagination is activated. I remember while attending a session at San Diego Comic-Con, the team from James Cameron's movie Avatar shared how it took over 10 years to take the movie from imagination to the big screen. When the team ran into technological roadblocks, they had to innovate solutions resulting in new technologies to the industry as a whole. Not only did their imaginations overcome tech issues to build a visually stunning fantasy world, but it also created a new language for the imagined inhabitants of that world as well.

When we are able to visualize ourselves successfully choosing the steps that lead us to where we want to go, our destination becomes a higher priority, and gratification relegates itself to a natural consequence of our arrival at that destination. However, we cannot hope to base our proactive approach solely on our perception of the future alone. There is one other place we need to use our time machine to travel to. Let's hit the rewind button to review the past. It's time to get uncomfortable.

Past (reflection)

There is a saying that hindsight is 20/20. What that saying fails to mention is that hindsight is only 20/20 if you pay attention to the lessons presented. At times, we must immerse ourselves in the past to seek out those lessons through a meditative process called reflection. Reflection is similar to visualization, but rather than looking ahead at future steps, we look back at the footprints left behind by the choices we have already made. Reflection helps develop proactive approaches because it allows us to scrutinize our prior actions while simultaneously pairing them with our presently known outcomes. The struggle I have found for myself and many other people that I have coached is figuring out how to reflect on the past without getting entangled in our previous failures. Rather than looking at the past as a lesson, we often weaponize it and use it to punish ourselves in the present. When executed properly, reflection should be an exercise defined in the establishment of discipline, not building regret.

When we jump into our time machine and visit the past, it is important to observe through both lenses of who we were at that point in time and who we are in the present. Sometimes those lenses will align, but often they will be two different perspectives. Healthy reflection involves being accountable for the roles that we played in our past to help make space for forgiveness and growth. Not being willing to admit our role in our greatest regrets can cause them to haunt us for a lifetime. Right before I go into a moment of reflection I give myself the same pep talk: "It's time to get uncomfortable." I go in knowing the person I presently am will more than likely have different thoughts and often better solutions than what was available to my past self. Even if that past was earlier that same day. The discomfort drives me to perform root-cause analysis about the event rather than symptom-based analysis.

As a young father, I have made more mistakes in raising my children than I care to count. One of the more recent mistakes that I revisited was the fact that I have not told my children that I am proud of them often enough. When I focus on the symptoms that drive this behavior, I look at things like being tired, having to correct them on behaviors that I am not proud of, and other excuses that hinder me from simply saying that I am proud of them. Though these symptoms may occur when I am not telling my children that I am proud of them, they are not the root cause. When I shift my focus from looking for who or what I can blame to the root cause I simplify the issue to one specific reason. I am not focused on giving my children praise about the things that I am proud of. Reflecting on missed opportunities with this direct truth creates an internal conflict between my shortcomings as their father and the father that I desire to be. Making excuses (focusing on symptoms) to address those paternal shortcomings is a more comfortable strategy to reconcile the feelings of guilt and shame that come with that truth, but it does not provide a solution to the actual issue. By reflecting on the past and my role in it, the question now becomes, how do I forgive myself for my shortcomings as a father so I can better identify opportunities to share my pride in my children with them? When we can forgive our previous decisions, we are able to glean more lessons from our past because we will spend more time looking at what could have made the outcome better rather than actually regretting our inability to change the outcome. These improved critical thinking skills can be applied to the present in order to create better solutions.

Present (Mindfulness)

As easy as it is for us to visit the past and future in our time machine, we never really live there. At all times we are in what Dr. Jon Kabat-Zinn of the Center for Mindfulness refers to as the infinite yet timeless state of the present. Embracing proactive approaches shines the brightest in the present when we learn how to implement the meditative practice of mindfulness. At its basic level, mindfulness is about being aware of the existence of the present. As we delve beyond the surface, we find that on a deeper level, mindfulness is about focusing intentionally on the now, while remaining non-judgmental about whatever it has to offer. In this space, we learn that our life is being experienced as our existence emerges in one continual fluid moment. So when it comes to proactive approaches, mindfulness helps shift us from a filtered judgment-based existence of suffering to an unfiltered experience of peace.

When I worked 3 jobs, I could always be found in 1 of 3 states. Coming, going, or sleeping. Due to the small window between my jobs, I never seemed to get enough of the third state, sleep. I would find myself at functions with family and friends, either sleeping in a corner or worse, awake, and disconnected. One day, between the time when I arrived at my home to change for work and the time when I had to leave to go to my next job, I had a 5-minute window to sleep. I knew immediately that 5 minutes would not be enough time to sleep, and it was this realization that allowed me to stumble across a solution. Rather than lying down with the intention of sleeping, I laid on my bed in the yoga corpse pose (flat on my back with palms facing the ceiling) and focused on rest, relaxation, and weightlessness. By accepting what the moment had to offer rather than judging its inadequate ability to provide sleep, I learned the importance of embracing rest. When I arose for work, I had alleviated my mind of a portion of my unnecessary exhaustion, lowered my anxiety, and ungrudgingly headed to my second job. Until that moment I had been so hyper-focused on the next thing I had to do (The Future), that I was never really present in my sleep as a form of mental rest.

I was introduced to mindfulness by a chance encounter with mental exhaustion, but in a lecture given at Brown University in April of 2019, Dr. Jon Kabat-Zinn provided an excellent place to begin practicing a similar exercise in mindfulness. Tomorrow morning, as you wake up before you grab your phone and scroll through social media or exit the bed to start your morning routine, I invite you to give yourself permission to try this exercise.

- **Passion Point:** How do you connect to the present?

Move into the yoga corpse pose. While lying on your back, inhale through your nose, and exhale through your mouth. As you breathe and without judgment, draw attention to your breathing. Intentionally focus on how your chest rises and falls, how the oxygen entering your lungs feels as it fills the present moment. Now move that attention to various parts of your body for about 5 - 60 seconds at a time. Your hands, feet, nose, shoulders, any part you choose. What do these parts feel? Do they tingle? Is there pain? Do they feel nothing? Do not attempt to imprint a new or desired experience on them or explain why they are in their present state. Simply meet them where they are and be present with them as is.

This exercise is recommended daily. As easy as this exercise may sound, don't be surprised if at first, you can only intentionally focus on the present for a few seconds before it is muddled by judgment, planning for the upcoming day, and other random thoughts. These thoughts are a lot like breathing, you don't have to think about them in order for them to take place. Unlike breathing, you will not die if you do not latch on to each thought that rises to the surface. Be patient as you develop this ability knowing that you wouldn't be able to lift 100 pounds your first day in the gym, and this exercise in mindfulness will not be any different.

The biggest part about the present that I have come to admire is that connecting to it connects us deeply to the feelings of gratitude and appreciation. Imagine driving down a highway with fields of beautiful wildflowers on each side of the road. As you drive, the groups of passing flowers appear to be uniform, almost an endless sea of color. But what happens if you slow down? You begin to see the individual flowers. If you pull over to the side of the road to observe the flowers closely, you find that each flower is endowed with its own form of unique beauty. No matter how fast or slow you are driving you can see the flowers as you drive, but until you actually stop, you have not truly experienced them. Our lives operate in a similar manner. If we speed through conversations, birthdays, and other experiences without ever slowing down or stopping, we miss the uniqueness of every moment that life has to offer.

As we strengthen our abilities to identify issues and embrace more proactive approaches, we will find that there are not as many urgent issues in our lives as we may have initially believed. By surrounding ourselves with fewer pressures to rapidly make decisions, we allow ourselves to intentionally procrastinate on instant gratification opportunities while expanding the reaction time we have to choose delayed gratification results. Remember to put first things first, and that overextending yourself, whether financially or mentally, can inadvertently cause what matters to you most to be at the mercy of what matters the least. There will certainly be some days that we find ourselves flirting with the idea of hiring back living beyond our means, but just be sure not to extend an offer of employment that you will later regret.

BILLY F. WROE JR.

CHAPTER 2

Just Enough Isn't Enough

f you have ever played sports competitively, then you know the importance of putting forth your maximum effort. National Football Museum Hall of Famer David Beckham, one of the greatest professional soccer players of all-time, was the first British player to win titles across 4 countries. He was quoted saying, "I have always believed that if you want to achieve anything special in life you have to work, work, and then work some more." It is not so much about the actual accolades that he amassed, but the work he put into obtaining them. Imagine if every time Beckham attempted to score a goal at practice, he kicked the ball with just enough force to move the ball across the goal line. He would not have developed the power necessary to score in a game, and he definitely never would have played soccer at an elite level. That was one lesson Coach Andre and Ms. Schroeder drilled into us at an early age during elementary basketball practice. We would perform how we practiced. Who knew they were really talking about life?

When trying to ignite our passion, just enough is not enough. In order to start a campfire, you don't just throw logs in a pit and light them on fire. You start by gathering some kindle (twigs, dead leaves, and grass) to initiate the fire. Once the spark ignites the fire, you add larger and larger sticks until you can begin adding logs. You don't just stop at kindle or jump straight to logs. There is a process. Just as kindle is enough to initiate a campfire, but not enough to sustain it, such is bare minimum effort. You might reach the beginning of success, but you will not be able to sustain it.

When it comes to our work ethic, if we adopt a bare minimum mentality, our goals will constantly live on the brink of failure due to an insufficient margin for error. I used to believe that my work ethic only pertained to the work that I actually performed at work. That I could somehow be driven during work activities and less driven during my personal activities. It was the age-old question of what came first, the chicken, or the egg? The only difference was that I was looking at the relationship between success and failure rather than poultry. Contrary to my belief, my poor work ethic from my personal life carried over into my professional life, not the other way around. If I showed up late to personal events, I showed up late to work. If I struggled to find balance in my household budget, I struggled to manage my workload in the office. A bare minimum mentality has a direct impact on our execution, and over a short period of time, it will stagnate the results of our passions. That is why it is our second job mentality that we will call into the office for termination.

Bare Minimum Mentality

The Bare Minimum Mentality happens when we take on the perspective of doing just enough not to fail, rather than doing everything that we can to succeed. Because the mindset is internal, without adequate time spent in reflection, we are left to identify the disorder based solely upon the symptoms reflected in our actions. Have you ever found yourself lying in bed, hitting the snooze button 15 times before you actually wake up with just enough time to get ready and out the door before you are late to work or school? What about putting off a college paper until the absolute last minute before an approaching deadline? We often consider these acts of procrastination as poor time management, or as I liked to refer to them during the denial phase, "Strategic Time Management." However, time is not the issue at all. It only feels like time is the issue because we have chosen to impart minimal effort so often that we no longer consider the role our own input plays as a determining factor. We see this in romantic relationships where one person can be well aware of what their partner wants from them but will only provide it right when things are about to fall apart, or after the relationship has already failed. There is only a willingness to provide just enough to see the relationship continue, but not enough to see it flourish. So what are the behaviors that drive us towards the bare minimum mentality? More importantly, what can we do to drive the mentality away from us? To answer these questions, let's look at how the bare minimum mentality operates within competition.

Playing to the Level of Others

In the financial investment industry the terms FIFO, FILO, LIFO, and LILO, are used to describe how an investor reconciles their investments. To keep it simple, no matter the acronym "F" represents the word First, "L" represents Last, and "I" & "O" represent In and Out. If an investor with a FILO investment strategy, has purchased the same stock at different times and wanted to sell some of the stock, the first stock that they purchased (First In) would be the last stock to be sold (Last Out). Have you ever worked for a company where you were FILO? Each day you watch people come into the office after you and leave before you. When we allow ourselves to have a bare minimum mentality, the allure to join at best the average and at worst the subpar can be very tempting. If we succumb to that temptation then we dilute our abilities and conform to our competitors' level. However, by choosing not to conform we can unlock 2 additional options for ourselves, either embrace the difference or evolve and compete.

Conform - Playing Down

We make the choice to conform to our competition when we choose to lower our personal standards to meet the perceived standards of competitors below it. Conformity never originates from a healthy place for an individual because it typically forces change through our internal interpretations of external fears. We almost always choose this strategy for one of three reasons: either a fear of missing out, fear of exile, or a fear of consequence. The beginning of my professional career was heavily saturated with call center employment. If you have ever worked in a call center, then you know that the number one reason for termination is adherence to the attendance policy. Early in my career I found myself acclimating to the average behaviors of my peers in these environments. Somehow when I would arrive at work on time and others would arrive late daily, I felt as if I was being left out of some type of special club. I figured that if they could earn about the same money with minimal effort put forth, then so could I. I started each job with great enthusiasm, but after about 3 months or so, I would begin to slowly shift my standards to that of my peers. Within a few months and on rare occasions in a little over a year, I would find myself on final disciplinary action due attendance adherence.

Conforming typically leads us to unintended but easily antic-ipated results. Even before I started to conform in the call center work environment, there were 3 things that stood out like the red on a baboon's backside. First, for many of us, this was not our first call center experience. In fact, the average number of previous call center employers for an employee was between 3 to 5 employers with about 6 months to 1 year of tenure at each. Second, as I said before, most of our pay was comparable to one another. Working at different call centers in the past did not put us into different tax brackets. The third thing was a little more subtle, but once the luster wore off of the new environment, I realized it was right at the surface all along. The majority of the people working in the chairs were simply there to exchange their life hours for an agreed upon hourly rate, and it was apparent that in doing so, they did not genuinely want to be there at all. So, what caused the allure of this group to resonate with me? What was the direct benefit I received by lowering my work ethic to the bare minimum?

Most of us are wired with an intrinsic desire to be socially connected. Even introverted personalities have this characteristic, they just display it differently than extroverted personalities. For me, conforming to the majority of the population ensured that my chances of establishing social connections was all but guaranteed. I was officially a part of the "In crowd." I was invited to lunches and outside work activities, and entrusted with confidential information on a regular basis. What I did not realize was that by dimming my professional light to fit in, I had inadvertently confined myself to roles below my actual abilities. I griped about my pay all the time, but made no effort to expand upon my value to the company. I frequently found out about opportunities that I would have been interested in as the person who was hired for the position was introduced to our team. I failed to communicate my desire to take on greater roles and responsibilities, all the while being completely ignorant to the reality that I was actually caught up in the typical conformity cycle. Conformity may work in high-school popularity contests, but in the adult world its price requires that you hide your authentic self and disappear into the masses. It is a price too high to pay if you are ever going to experience your passion raw and uncut. It became critical to unlock a new option, but I had to start small.

Embrace the Difference (Stand Your Ground)

My years spent as a Technical Recruiter were some of the most developmental in building my professional acumen. It was in this role that I began to learn how to sedate the temptation of mediocrity. The specific term that removed the veil from my peers' performance was stack rank. For those who have never heard this term before, it simply means that employees are prioritized by either their company or manager in order of most important (mission critical) to least important (expendable). When you perform a stack ranking exercise, no 2 people sit at the same level. Even if 2 individuals possess the same value, they are compared until one is above and one is below. In a sales organization, your stack rank determines your fate more times than not. Who has access to which clients, how compensation disbursement is structured, what rules apply, all of these corporate politics flow through the filter of our stack rank.

Timeout: Stack Ranking

Grab your **Passion Journal**. Think about the team you are working on right now. If the team has hundreds of people, dwindle that number down to your immediate sphere with a maximum of 12 coworkers (be sure to include yourself). Beginning with the number 1 (highest importance), stack rank each team member. Write notes as to how you decided to prioritize each individual. Remember, this is not a popularity contest, but solely about the perceived value of each individual as they correspond to the company. It is ok to be brutally honest.

Once you have every team member ranked, divide the total team count by 3. Round that result up to the next whole number (ex. if you have 7 team members your result would be 3) and place a red X by the name of that many of the lowest ranked employees. Take the next lowest ranked employees and place a circle next to the name of that many employees. At this point only the top employees should not have anything next to their names.

Where did you fall in the list? What was next to your name? Those names with a red X are the employees that would have the highest probability for termination if the company decided to execute a layoff tomorrow. The employees with the circle next to their name are on the bubble. These employees could possibly be terminated or keep their job, depending on how much money the company is attempting to save. Lastly, there are the employees that have nothing next to their names. Though these employees are not on the bubble, even they can be in jeopardy of termination, under the right set of unfortunate circumstances.

Now look at your rank and determine if that is where you wanted to be. Would you even have a chance at retaining your job? Do you have the potential to score even higher? What can you do to challenge yourself at your current level? Take these insights and write out some goals to improve your rank in one specific way before your next evaluation.

Though you are measuring yourself against others, always remember that you are your competition. You are attempting to outdo you, and sometimes outdoing others happens to be a byproduct of that activity. You can do this exercise with any group of people that you engage with, it does not have to only apply to the work environment. As you improve your value, revisit this exercise often to measure your progress.

Though I understood the concept of stack ranking, it took some time before I became efficient enough to use it to my advantage. At the end of 2009 during the Great Recession, I found myself back in the call center world working for a regional logistics company. I came in with the idea that I could outperform the majority of my peers by doing the one thing that I knew would not come easily to most, adhere to the attendance policy. I came in with the best intentions, but it was not long before I found myself flirting with that bare minimum mentality of conforming to the masses and I earned myself a verbal warning. I had a choice to make, either I could continue down the cyclical path or I could stand my ground and embrace the fact that I was different, and wanted to be that way. I chose to climb off the hamster wheel, regroup and begin my ascent up the corporate ladder. This would undoubtedly be a marathon and not a sprint.

In the beginning, deciding to maintain behaviors that would allow me to promote was a lonely process. Besides my inner motivations, I had to recruit some additional forces to help me create the bridge that led from my current circumstances to my desired future. One of the inspirational speakers I listened to daily was Brian Tracy. Mr. Tracy's videos resonated with me because he often spoke about the kaizen principle. In fact, my personal mantra was established based on this very same concept. Kaizen is a combination of two Japanese words, kai (improvement) and zen (good). Unlike English, many languages around the world place the adjective after the noun. So what is a good improvement? It is a continual process of conjoined incremental improvements. This is the very essence of how you condition your mind in order to stand your ground. By doing so, each day presents an opportunity to either not slide back or to inch forward. Eventually, days become months and inches of progress collectively become feet. Kaizen feels great when you are inching forward, but the first day that you have to fight just to stay in the same place you never forget.

- **Passion Point:** What areas are you challenging yourself to grow in daily?

I was about 6 months into standing my ground on displaying the behaviors that I felt added to my professional value. All of a sudden another supervisor was hired and once again I had not even been considered. This time there was a little extra sting in the venom. In addition to the supervisor role being filled under my nose, my department's bonuses were taken away as well. I remember asking myself, "Why even bother to try to grow professionally?" Believe me, bare minimum was right there ready to comfort me with open arms. We often take these disappointing times and create toxic behaviors that move us even further from our goals. How many times have you heard yourself say, "If they paid me more money I would do better work"? That is like saying that you would be a better boyfriend if your partner loved you more.

After I processed the emotions of disappointment, I started to think about how Mr. Tracy talked about his ability to double his income and none of those tools involved retreat. Co-Founder Cory Strong of Dirty Soles Footwear Group, a Black-Owned business out of Newark, NJ, made it simple and plain when he shared a short story about quitting versus perseverance. When you've walked halfway across the street barefoot on a hot summer day to play with the kids on the other side of the street, it is in the moment when you realize that your feet are burning on the hot asphalt that you have a choice to make. You can either retreat back to the safety of the cool grass or run to the other side. "We teach our children that retreat is not an option." We will inevitably arrive at this point in the pursuit of our passion and this is where we take notice of the discomfort and the questions begin. In that same spirit as Mr. Strong articulated, I doubled down on my growth and committed to making the next promotion mine. I went to the director of the call center and asked for a meeting to discuss what would be needed for me to be considered for the next opportunity. In doing so I received a clear understanding on what my 6 months of activity lacked: concise direction, such as taking the initiative to learn about other parts of the business and seizing organic leadership opportunities in the interim. It was the difference between launching a rocket into space versus launching that same rocket specifically to the moon. I solidified my stance and the next stage of moving out of the bare minimum mentality was primed to begin. The incremental changes I made in my professional cocoon were ready to evolve.

Evolution Adapt - Playing Up, Not to Others But to Self

Bob Iger, CEO of Disney was quoted saying, "Never accept mediocrity if there's still an opportunity to make something better." It is this mentality that has driven the success of the company by making decisions like acquiring Marvel, Fox News, and developing the streaming platform Disney Plus. This quote is true no matter if it is applied to a company and their products or if we apply it to our own lives where we are the actual product. One might think that this is where I started to compete with others above my skill level to improve myself, but that is the mistake that many make which leads them right back to the beginning of the conformity cycle. When I began to mature out of the bare minimum mentality, I stopped looking at others as my competitors and began looking at myself as my sole competition. Don't get me wrong, you can glean characteristics from people above your level through mentorship and adapt them to suit your purposes, but that does not mean that you have to compete at their level. The decision we make to evolve will define our competition paradox which is how long-term growth is established and sustained.

A paradox is an event that takes place when we perceive that our hand is forced by the circumstances that proceed it. While at the same time, the choice we feel that the circumstance "forces" us to choose, creates a perpetual cycle of the original circumstances. This paradox becomes dangerous when attached to others, because it makes other people the bar of which you are attempting to exceed. When you run out of people to compete with, you eventually settle into a state of complacency. As Bill Watterson would say, "The problem with people is that they're only human." When your competitive focal point is someone else, sometimes that person does not show up physically, mentally, or both, which means that simply outperforming them may deliver subpar results.

As a decent recreational basketball player, I have played thousands of hours of pick-up ball games during my life. For many years I noticed while on the court, I always played to the level of the team that I was playing against. If the team was really good, I moved faster, played tighter defense, and was more aggressive on offense. On the opposite end of the spectrum, if my opponents lacked skill, I was lazy coming up the court, allowing them to breeze by when they were on offense assuming that they'd miss their shot anyway, and my own shots were ridiculous at best. These mirroring and matching behaviors made my skills appear and feel inconsistent. It was not until I found myself on the court alone, walking through the process of driving and shooting with my left hand, focusing on my foot placement, and honing my consistency through repetition that I actually improved my game based on my own skill level. This changed how I saw the game as a generic opportunity to win, to a specific moment to put into action what I had practiced in isolation. I did not know it until years later, but I had stumbled across a healthy competition paradox that I could carry far beyond the game of basketball.

Your best chance to establish a healthy competition paradox is by investing your energy in a competitor who is going to show up everyday regardless of the conditions: yourself. By making yourself the focal point of your competition, you continually reinvent the person that you are working to outperform which doesn't allow complacency the space it needs to take root. You will regularly be forced to innovate solutions to overcome the challenges that held you back from achieving additional greatness. Fast forward 6 months after initiating efforts aligned with the concise direction I was provided by the director of customer service, where did this evolution lead? I was offered not only a lead position in the customer service department, but I was also presented with an opportunity to move into cost analysis as an entry level analyst.

When we lose sight of who our true competition is, doing just enough to meet the bare minimum is a very comfortable place to be. However, while we rest on our laurels, we also drift further away from embracing the full effect of our passions. In order to close the gap, we are required to commit to putting forth a maximum effort, and in doing so, we will set new heights to ascend to. Take a moment today to stop in a mirror and look yourself directly in the eyes. Put yourself on notice that minimum is no longer acceptable, that your passion is on the horizon, and that you will be coming for yourself every single day. I guarantee that you will push past the ceiling of mediocrity and the bare minimum behaviors that you once extended offer letters to will become unemployable.

CHAPTER 3

Time is of the Essence

t was Sunday, May 26, 2002, and the Sacramento Kings were playing against the Los Angeles Lakers in game 4 of the NBA Western Conference Finals. Going into the game Sacramento had the opportunity to extend their 2 - 1 lead in the series. Sacramento dominated early in the game, but LA fought back to bring the game to within 2 points (99 - 97 Sacramento) with 11 seconds left in the fourth quarter. LA had possession of the ball and it was known that they would put the ball into the hands of one of the greatest NBA players of all time, Kobe Bryant. Kobe aggressively attacked the basket, but missed his layup. Shaq made an unsuccessful attempt to tip the ball back in. In an effort to put another attempt out of reach, Vlade Divac (Sacramento's center) slapped the ball out to the top of the key where Robert Horry (LA's power forward) recovered the ball. Realizing that there was less than one second left on the game clock, Horry immediately shot a 3 pointer. Time expired while the ball was in the air, and as the ball hit the bottom of the net, Laker fans erupted. The game ended with a final score of 100 - 99, LA. It was a moment that happened almost 20 years ago, but as a Sacramento native, I remember it vividly.

Horry had the benefit of a shot clock which helped him to understand the gravity of the game-time situation. He did not have time to pass the ball, drive to the basket, or call a timeout. He only had time to shoot. Unlike Horry in the game, we are born with an invisible shot clock. Actually, it is a two-sided clock. On one side, the clock adds every second, minute, and hour of our life. On the opposite side, the clock has a timer that is counting down towards the end of our life's journey. We can only see the side that is adding up our time as it unfolds, but the side counting down does not reveal itself until every second has passed. Even though we know this, many of us still play with our time as if we not only know how much is left in our coffers, but how much time others have as well. As such, we regularly sacrifice what is most important for lesser priorities. This will be the next behavior we call into the office for termination.

Sacrificing What is Most Important

Sacrificing what is most important occurs when less important matters begin to occupy their space. As we rationalize why this behavior is acceptable, it simultaneously becomes normalized. Maybe our parents taught us that our dreams were a waste of time and we needed to be more practical. Our mental health in the form of depression, anxiety, or feelings of inadequacy can all have a negative impact on our ability to set appropriate priorities. We could be overwhelmed by the importance of our image and invest every moment that we have available into the pursuit of success. Whatever the excuse, over time this lopsided relationship can create deeply rooted habits that erode the foundation in which our passion is to be built upon.

I once sat in on a sales meeting where one of the agents bragged about how for a year straight he spent no significant time with his family (wife and children) to make $160k. He said that they had to sacrifice so he could give them the life that they wanted. What do you think was really happening? I am almost positive that if you asked his family to make a choice to either have him present in the household or receive $10k a month for a year (which is about what $160k is after taxes) they would choose the former and not the later. While he prioritized giving them the life that they allegedly wanted, he moved what was most important, giving them him, to the sideline. In reality, the family did not choose to sacrifice, he sacrificed himself on their unrequested behalf. What is worse is that in order to achieve the outcome again, the same sacrifice or more would need to be made the following year. His boisterous tone made it appear as if he was excited for round 2.

In Japan, occupational related deaths have occurred on such a frequent basis that they created a term for it. Karoshi. These deaths are not categorized as work-related accidents. Rather, karoshi refers to a person literally working themselves to death. No wonder why in Bonnie Ware's *The Top Five Regrets of the Dying: A Life Transformed by the Dearly Departing*, the second most prevalent regret was "I wish I didn't work so hard." I have never heard of a person on their death-bed wishing for more work, more money, more status, or even more material possessions. Regardless of what the regret may be in our final moments of life, the remedy to it is always found in how we allocate our time. Since we don't know how much time we are going to receive, *memento mori*, which is Latin for "Remember you must die." Let's start defining what matters most in our life in order to set our priorities accordingly.

Determine What Matters Most

Two times in my life, I have missed the opportunity to talk to friends by one phone call before they unexpectedly passed away. These moments caused deep feelings of regret because I knew that in not taking their final calls I assumed that they had plenty of time left on their shot clock. Had I known that these would be my last opportunities to say what I wanted to say, hear their voices, or even simply spend time with them, how different would my actions have been? Similar to the stack ranking exercise we discussed in chapter 2, determining what matters most is an exercise in which we compare and contrast our life priorities. Sounds simple enough. Who doesn't know what their priorities are, right? Well, in a blog titled "30 Home-invading Work-Life Balance Statistics for 2020" on Healthcareers.co, 48% of Americans considered themselves to be workaholics, 66% of

American workers lacked work-life balance, and 26% of Americans took their work home with them. According to these statistics, it would seem that work matters the most. Though this is a true statement, how it is presented is only partially correct.

The assumption that work matters the most becomes flawed when we only apply it to one's employment. In essence, what the previous statistics convey is that for almost half of all working Americans, employment mattered more than anything else in their life. That is not to be confused with employment being the only thing that mattered, but behind breathing, eating, and going to the bathroom, it is a strong contender, even against sleep. When I say that work matters the most, I am referring to the focused energy that we pour into all areas of our life, not just our professions. Working with my children in an effort to build a stronger paternal bond, working with a friend to help them get through a difficult time, or even working with myself to improve my understanding of my purpose are all aspects of work. However, working in these instances becomes an investment worthy of our most valuable currency, time. My sons' godfather and I frequently remind each other of the importance of protecting those types of investments.

- **Passion Point:** What is a worthy investment of your time?

If you came to this chapter looking for a universal formula on setting priorities, I have bad news for you. There isn't one. In fact, as I researched different methods to compare against my own process, I found that any attempt to standardize the approach to establishing priorities lacked the personal intimacy necessary to implement it in the real world. What is important to one person may be completely irrelevant to another person. The good news is that all of this is ok, because our process is meant to be personal and unique to us. No matter what we prioritize or the approach we decide to take, the process will always require us to be completely honest about what we want for our life, and more importantly, what we want from it.

Think about the "For-your-life" question as your life's outcome/legacy. What do you want your feelings to be if you have the opportunity to reflect on your life as a whole towards the end of it? What do you want to leave behind for others to evaluate about your life in your absence? The "From-your-life" question is more about each step in the journey. What do you want to experience along the way? Whether your answer is health, relationships, religious beliefs, bank account balances, upcoming events, etc., who's to say that those priorities are incorrect? Even if other people feel that your priorities are out of order, they're only measuring against their own personal priorities which can at times be internally skewed.

- **Passion Point:** What do you consider to be the highest priority in your life right now?

Compromised Priorities

When my first son, Ezekiel was born, I remember the overwhelming feelings of love and responsibility that I felt the first time I looked at him. I knew that there was nothing that I would not do for him. What used to matter most to me abruptly shifted away from me to him. There was an upside to this newfound priority as it rapidly pushed me into maturity as a young father. However, at times what I prioritized as maturing for his sake also enabled me to double down on a few unhealthy decisions as well. Our internal skewing of priorities occurs naturally as we learn how to manage the pressures of life. I did not know it until later in life regarding my son, but my compass had been emotionally compromised and it needed to be recalibrated.

Check-in & Checkout

Unlike the set-it-and-forget-it cooking gadgets found on the internet, our priorities are not static. In fact, I would wager that our priorities are dynamic in nature and they fluctuate throughout the course of most days. Just as a hotel guest can choose the check-in and checkout dates of their stay, we get to choose the lifespan of our priorities. Sometimes a priority can stay for a weekend in the form of a homework assignment, cleaning the house, or even attending an event. Other times priorities may last for many years to a lifetime. Because our priorities can be compromised at any time, they should be evaluated frequently. However, similar to the additional cost a guest would incur if they wanted to extend their stay in their hotel room, we pay an additional cost when we refuse to reprioritize. Especially when a priority's current level of importance has diminished or expired.

Over Correction

Have you ever known a person who stayed in a relationship too long? Did that person come out on the other side with a list of "never-again" statements that hindered their next relationship? When we create new standards during heightened states, disappointment, hurt, or even happiness, we tend to overcorrect. In the same manner, our outdated priorities can also cause us to overreact and dramatically swing the pendulum from the far left to the far right. If we came from poverty, we may refuse to downgrade our priority to earn income. If we had parents that were controlling during our childhood, we may rebel in adulthood and overly exclude them from providing advice and guidance. This overcorrection of prioritization is what happened when I became a new father. I swung straight past the middle that allowed both my son and I to be important and straight to him being everything. Gaining a genuine understanding of the pressures that led me to this imbalance also led me to embrace my current highest priority to-date. The importance of and my responsibility to maintain my peace.

Regardless of your personal formula, the byproduct of proper prioritization is always peace. As the old African proverb goes, "A man who never recognizes his mistakes will never know peace." As we begin to move lesser important matters towards the back, it may feel like we have to make difficult decisions. However, as we apply the knowledge we gain from our experiences, the burden of making those decisions begins to lift. By learning the difference between temporal disruptions to our state of peace versus the ongoing disturbances that almost feel like an unending assault, we empower ourselves to move from reactive-based prioritization to objective-based prioritization.

I use peace to gauge how well my priorities are functioning for me because I have found that if I can see peace at the end of a process that might be stressful or uncomfortable, I am likely to take actions that keep me focused on the objective and not the journey. Peace of mind, peace in a relationship, financial peace, whatever peace I believe awaits on the other side of adversity, I am willing to move mountains to achieve it. In the absence of peace we find war. If happiness is your priority and you are not at peace, then in one way or another you are at war with unhappiness. How you fight that war will determine if you are victorious or create additional wars.

Synthetic Solutions

On my father's side of the family I have seen firsthand the impact that heavy drug abuse can have on the lives of people that I loved and cared about. I often think about how desperate you must become to intentionally expose your body to poison in order to feel, or in some instances not feel at all. Drug addiction is not an illness that only affects my family. The statistics for drug abuse in America are staggering. One of the most shocking things about the numbers is that adolescents age 12 and up are included in many of the categories from tobacco, to marijuana, to more addictive substances like cocaine, heroin, and meth. These synthetic solutions can take on other non-drug related forms such as gambling, pornography, shopping, video games, sports, and even people. Any category that a person can lean on as a crutch has the potential of becoming a synthetic solution. Make sure that as you realign your priorities that you do not enter into a second war and quickly find yourself overrun.

You Can't Fake it 'til You Make it

It is easy to say our priorities out loud, but much harder to live them. Finding the balance that works for you will be an ongoing exercise in trial and error. Take a moment today to reflect on your priorities and the outcomes that they are producing. Are you living them or just preaching them? Are they producing peace or chaos? No matter what your personal priorities are or how they are organized, at the end of the day it is important for us to realize that we are not sacrificing priorities at all. We are sacrificing time. Always remember that your invisible shot clock is constantly ticking until the end of the game. Expend as much energy as you can to garner the best from your life's journey while building a monument worthy of your life's legacy. Live an intentional life and avoid the complacency that comes with taking it for granted. Allow the small things to be small, and the great things to be great. And no matter what, never be afraid to take a shot.

CHAPTER 4

Dreams are Supposed to Live Outside of the Box

We all know the fairytale of the 3 little pigs and the big bad wolf. Instead of the traditional story that focuses on 3 pigs, I want you to imagine that there is only 1 pig with 3 houses. Each house represents an attempt at success and the wolf represents the adversities we encounter in life. As the story goes, the pig's first two attempts at success fail when faced with adversity. However, in the third attempt, the pig finally builds a strong enough structure to endure the adversity that comes with the wolf's huffing and puffing, achieves success, and throws a party for all of his friends to come to see his house made of bricks. The reason I remove 2 pigs from the story is that 3 pigs make it seem as if all we have to do is work hard 1 time and we can be successful. I add the party with friends because that is how most of us operate with failure and success. No one was invited to the house of straw or sticks, but as soon as the house of bricks is successful we want the world to see it.

Woodrow Wilson eloquently articulated the importance of public failures when he stated, "You are not here merely to make a living. You are here in order to enable the world to live more amply, with greater vision, with a finer spirit of hope and achievement. You are here to enrich the world, and you impoverish yourself if you forget the errand." We enrich the world's spirit by sharing with it both our successes and failures. When people feel as if failure is unique to them, despair can set in. Misery does not like the company because it wants other people to be miserable, it simply does not want to be alone. Unsolicited extended isolation can be a very scary place for anyone, especially when you feel like you are the only one making mistakes. With that in mind, it is time to call our last behavior into the office. Hiding failures, our employer-employee relationship comes to an end here.

Hiding Failures

If you recall from chapter 1, the stories that we create about the unknown future guide our disciplines. Hiding our failures occurs when we allow fear-based stories regarding failure to limit our willingness to be exposed. Look at it like this. The first lie that any of us ever told was more than likely during our childhood. Why did we choose to lie? In its purest form, we chose an action that was incorrect (failure) and did not want to get in trouble for it (exposure). Our first dance with hiding our failure does not seem too bad, but the mind is like nutrient-rich soil, capable of growing whatever behaviors we choose to sow with very little effort. Practice makes us better, and over time hiding our failure from others can quickly transition into hiding failures from ourselves. However, when we dare to be vulnerable, we can use failure to quickly unlock 3 secrets that will later support our passion.

Failure Presents an Opportunity to Improve (Secret 1)

Outside of our mind's ability to shield us from traumatic events, Alzheimer's, and grandiose delusional disorders, we all typically know the truth. When we begin to willingly hide failures from ourselves we are choosing to accept denial. Though the immediate relief from not having to process the failure may appear beneficial, negligence often comes at a much higher cost. I remember when my older sister received her first car. It was a hand-me-down 1980's Toyota Corolla from our parents. I cannot recall how long it took, but I remember the engine locked up because she drove the car without oil in it. As with all cars, there were a couple of signs that failure was on the horizon. The place where my sister parked the car often had oil stains on the ground from an oil leak. At some point both the low-oil light and check-engine light lit up on the dashboard. Lastly, in the final moments leading up to the engine lock up, it began making noises, the thermostat gauge showed that it was overheating, until it finally just stopped running all together. A problem that started as a couple hundred dollars became a couple of thousand dollars. This is exactly what happens when we try to hide our failure from ourselves, we bury warning sign after warning sign, and ultimately pay in the form of catastrophic failure.

Timeout: Failure Opportunities

*Grab your **Passion Journal**. Take a moment to write down four of your most recently experienced failures. For this exercise, it does not matter whether the failures were public or private. Select one failure from the list to perform a deep dive on. What were some of the warning signs that presented prior to the failure occurring? Were there any warning signs that you chose to ignore or not take seriously? Get intimate with the opportunities you had to either avoid the failures or at least speed up the failure process. If you cannot identify opportunities, what did you learn from the failures? I am not referring to the heightened emotionally-compromised lessons, but the healthy tools you gained from the experiences. In this exercise, really attempt to separate the fat from the meat. Write down each insight that you are able to identify. You are going to use these insights to develop a strategy designed to intentionally disrupt the loop between your actions, failures, and lessons. This is a living list that will grow as you experience new failures and gain additional insights throughout your life, so keep them in a place where they will be readily available.*

I am a firm believer that we continually revisit the same issues in our life until we learn the lessons that we are intended to learn. Why? Because you cannot repair that which you ignore. When we choose an action that results in failure and refuse to acknowledge that failure or reject the healthy lessons from the experience, without luck, we become destined to make the same decisions that led us to the original outcome, failure. I refer to this process as the Action - Failure - Lesson Loop. Breaking this loop requires both the acknowledgment of failure and acceptance of lessons it teaches.

In 2016, South Korea company Samsung released their much-anticipated phone the Note 7. More than 2.5 million phones were purchased by consumers. Shortly after its market debut, reports of exploding batteries started topping national news headlines. A software failsafe designed to keep the phone battery from overheating failed and resulted in the battery spontaneously exploding. At one point the issue was so bad that Note 7 phones were banned by airlines. Samsung had a major public failure on their hands. Acknowledgement of the battery failure came in the form of a massive recall of all Note 7s. Shortly after the recall, Samsung took the lessons they learned from the recalled product to create a comprehensive 8-Point Battery Safety Check procedure for all of their products going forward. This process included simple steps such as durability testing and visual inspection, to much more sophisticated testing like the total volatile organic compound test used to ensure that there was no possibility for the volatile compounds within the battery to leak. Imagine if Samsung decided to just ignore the device failure and allowed batteries to continue to explode until consumer confidence was completely eroded. How would they be able to ever sell another product under those conditions?

It was the combination of Samsung's willingness to acknowledge the Note 7's battery issue while gleaning lessons from that failure, which unlocked the first secret of failure for them. Failure presents us with an opportunity to improve. By unlocking this secret, Samsung was able to improve their process, but more importantly regain consumer confidence, and put the failure behind them. The good news is that because failure is an ever-present possibility, improvement is an ever present opportunity.

Unlike Samsung, most of us don't have multi-million dollar failures looming in the shadows. However, in order for us to move past our own personal exploding phone era, whatever that may be in our life, we are going to have to learn how to draw out the opportunities that failure provides. By acknowledging our failures we reveal the lessons capable of disrupting the Action - Failure - Lesson Loop long enough to break the cycle. Of greater benefit, is that when those lessons are embraced, they empower us to overcome similar circumstances in order to avoid future failures.

Failure Presents an Opportunity for Others to Help (Secret 2)

When I refer to making your failures public, I am not saying that you have to stand on the busiest corner in New York City shouting out to random strangers about how you have failed. Exposing our failures is more so about exposing our dreams! When we attempt to hide our failure we simultaneously dim our light. Whether you want to speak into the lives of youth, share a form of artistry, start a business, or whatever your dreams are, when people know what your ambitions are, they also gain the ability to see whether or not those dreams are achieved. No, everyone is not entitled to know about your dreams, but you will be surprised at the allies you can acquire along the way to achieving your dreams through transparency.

When I put in my notice to resign from my first role as an analyst, I did not know what my next job would be, but I knew that going back to call center work was not an option I was willing to entertain. I could have quietly shifted from employed to unemployed, and no one would have been none the wiser. Instead, I decided to share with people that my current position had failed (notice I did not say that I failed). In making that decision I unwittingly unlocked the second secret of failure. When other people are aware of failures it gives them an opportunity to provide assistance, because they want to see you succeed. Surprisingly, 5 hours and about 20 job leads later, I received one that seemed to be in the goldilocks zone and began the process that led to my next job.

Contrary to how we believe that people are going to respond to our failures, when we have the right tribe surrounding us things are almost never as bad as we imagine that they will be. Yes, there will be those who attempt to tear you down in your lowest moments, but do your best to focus on your supporters and not the detractors. What you will find is that you will move further and further away from the fear-based story and realize that people don't think less of you at all. If anything, they hold you in a higher regard because of the trust that transparency instills. Rapport established at this level allows ideas to flow unimpeded by the fear of judgement.

Imagine that a building is on fire and someone is trapped on the fifteenth floor. As firefighters search the floor, they call out to the person that they are there to help. They have all the tools to take the person to where that person wants to be, safety, but out of fear the individual stays hidden and quiet. Eventually the firefighters move on, not because they don't want to help, but because they have been made to believe that assistance is not needed. When we hide our failures, we in essence are hiding ourselves from potential solutions that others have acquired from their experiences. Even worse, sometimes our own failures hold solutions for others who are at the beginning of their journey. Acknowledgement of our failures could help our peers avoid the pitfalls that we've already encountered. Think about all the resources that were poured into the effort to develop a vaccine during the 2020 Covid-19 pandemic. When something didn't work or a test vaccine was discontinued it was announced. In fact, scientists approached the challenge from so many angles that they decided to share their findings daily with the scientific community. This leap-frog approach led to the record-breaking development of the Covid vaccine. Previously, the fastest that we moved a vaccine from development to deployment was a 4-year time period. By sharing information (failures included), the Covid vaccine shortened that timeframe to less than a year.

In the same manner in which scientists came together during the pandemic, we can lean on those ahead of our process. There will be no shortcuts on the road to your passion, however, you can save time along the way. Create intentional spaces in your journey to sit with your predecessors to learn as much as you can from their experiences. Use their experiences to map out your predicted path to fully experiencing your own passion. Be a good steward of what you learn by continuing to pay forward both the knowledge you acquire from them and of that which is gained from your own personal journey.

Failure Liberates Us (Secret 3)

Somewhere between childhood and adulthood, I picked up a fear of heights. Not in the sense of climbing ladders or riding roller coasters, but when I am hundreds of feet in the air where I can see the space between me and the ground, let's just say that my heart rate becomes significantly elevated and I feel weakness in my stomach and knees. The fear-based stories that failure creates can stimulate similar feelings of dread and despair causing us to establish fear-inspired boundaries that limit our limitless potential. Just so we are clear, it is going to be extremely difficult to flourish in our passion while allowing our fears to stifle its growth.

We all know someone who is always saying what they are going to do, until it comes time to actually do it. I was guilty of doing this when it came to writing this book for years. Each time I would begin, judgmental thoughts about how it would be received echoed throughout my mind. I feared that I had not arrived yet to a place where I could advise others on their journey. Two things changed that allowed me to move past this roadblock. The first was that I realized that I was not telling anyone that they had to do anything. More so, I was sharing my story in hopes that my experiences would help them gain traction with their own dreams. The second was that I was never going to arrive at any worthy destination that would validate me for my destiny. Before, during, and after the completion of this book, failure would still be something that I experience from time to time. So in order to make progress I was going to have to lean on my strategy for creating a fearless mindset capable of overcoming the fear induced paralysis that failure can incite.

The more we interact with an activity the more familiar it becomes, helping our mind's reaction to the activity become more and more balanced. If you have a fear of public speaking, the more you speak publicly, the more comfortable you will become with it. The more you cook your own meals, the better the meals you cook for yourself taste (hopefully). This doesn't mean that you won't have some of the same anxieties, but you will understand that it is not as bad as your initial thoughts make it out to be. For me, in spite of my fear of heights, I attempt to interact with heights well beyond my comfort zone frequently. As a result of this desensitization strategy, on one cool May morning in 2009, I found myself connected in tandem, preparing to jump out of a perfectly good airplane.

I was completely fine until the plane door opened and we began moving towards the opening. In all honesty, it is probably best that the person I was attached to was responsible for making us jump. I might have allowed my fears to entrap me in inaction, but as we jumped out of the plane the third secret to failure was unlocked. Overcoming failure or the fear-based story that we imagine, often liberates us from their bondage. The moment I was out of the plane and in the sky, I felt the freedom of falling as the air rushed against my skin, and experienced one of the most amazing views I had ever seen of the California Valley. In that moment, I felt if it was possible for me to conquer the fear of all the potential failures that could take place in order for me to hit the ground, I could overcome anything, including the obstacles that stood in the way of my passions.

The Magic of Inspiration

The 3 secrets of failure are not often recognized during our difficulties. However, if we want to achieve something extraordinary in our lives, failure is a critical part of that journey. Whether we are inspiring ourselves or others, the magic of inspiration is found in our ability to overcome failure. When something is effortless it becomes easy to take for granted. Oppositely, when something comes at a cost, we value it more. We may have to hold some private struggles close to the chest, but whenever we fail, we must understand that sharing that failure helps everyone, especially us.

Chadwick Boseman's speech at Howard University is one of the most powerful examples of how we marry our failures and passions together. Boseman shared how the principles and standards that he learned at Howard University in essence, closed some doors to him early in his acting career. At one point he was fired from a prominent soap opera for speaking up about the stereotypical nature of his character. That failure early in his career did not take away from his success. In fact, it highlighted it. In spite of being fired from his first on-screen appearance in Hollywood, he went on to perform leading roles in movies such as *42 (The Jackie Robinson Story)*, *Get on Up (The James Brown Story)*, *Marshall (The Thurgood Marshall Story)*, and King T'Challa aka The Black Panther in *Black Panther*. Boseman went on to say, "Sometimes you need to feel the pain and sting of defeat to activate the real passion and purpose that God predestined inside of you." That is exactly what failure does when you allow it to empower you to move forward. When we stop hiding our dreams, they become limitless. Only then can our process for interviewing our passions truly begin.

BILLY F. WROE JR.

THE INTERVIEWS
(A Foundation for Your Passion)

CHAPTER 5

Your Passion has an Identity

G rowing up, one of my favorite childhood games was Hide and Go Seek. It didn't matter whether I was frantically searching for the perfect hiding place, or chasing after my friends as they attempted to reach the safety of the base, I literally played the game for hours at a time. I enjoyed the game so much that I played it well into my late 20s, upping the ante by playing at night in larger parks, and taking greater risks to find the optimal hiding place. In many ways, discovering our passion is a lot like playing a life-long game of hide and go seek. Our gifts (the hiders) start off tucked away in the perfect hiding places, while our experiences (the seeker) naturally seek out the locations of each gift. Each time an experience reveals a hiding place and we pursue our gift, we potentially add another piece of the puzzle to uncovering our passion. Over time, these pieces help us to define our intrinsic reconciliation process, or our Passion Identity. However, if we neglect a discovered gift long enough, it can slip back into hiding and the game of hide and go seek starts all over again. So how do we identify and retain the pieces that make up our Passion Identity?

Passion Identity

There is an old saying that "if it looks like a duck, and clucks like a chicken, then it is probably a chicken dressed up as a duck."

Ok, so I just made that up, but let me explain how this relates to our passion identity. Our Passion Identity is made up of 2 complex emotions: fulfillment and unfulfillment. Choices that result in feelings of fulfillment reinforce the likelihood that we will repeat the choice when given the same or similar circumstances to choose it again. While choices that result in feelings of unfulfillment produce a negative correlation that guide us away from making the same choices. These 2 emotions are considered complex because they consist of multiple emotions that can be either basic or complex in nature, and range within varying levels of intensity.

When we are fulfilled by a meal, we can feel a blend of our emotions surrounding happiness, excitement, calm, security, and even optimism. Each emotion plays its part in creating the complex emotion of fulfillment. We could experience happiness about the fact that we have eaten. Our excitement can originate from the type of food we have consumed. Calm can come in the form of sedating our initial physiological indicators of hunger. We then begin to feel security from having the knowledge that there was food available when it was needed. Lastly, due to our ability to meet the immediate need, optimism about additional food being available in the future can round out the emotion of fulfillment created by the meal. In the same way that a meal can evoke fulfillment, emotions derived from our choices and actions can help us establish resonance with our Passion Identity through the repetitive process of positive reinforcement.

Positive Reinforcement

Positive reinforcement is such a powerful tool because it solidifies our relationship with our Passion Identity by deepening our connection with the outcomes that fulfill us. In a way, we use positive reinforcement's quid-pro-quo (this for that) relationship to build resonance with our passion. It is not that our passion does not require work, but no matter what the cost is, the non-monetary benefit that we derive from our passion drives us to continually desire to interact with it. Contrarily, when actions are not positively reinforced, we build dissonance with our Passion Identity. In his book *The Happiness Advantage*, author Shawn Anchor shared how when activities in the workplace lack happiness, our overall performance suffers. To make things even more complex, between building resonance and dissonance, from time-to-time an activity that feels emotionally familiar can be misinterpreted as a passionate activity. This misinterpretation can lead to false positives in what we perceive our Passion Identity to be. Let's look at how we can become clear on whether the type of activities we are interacting with are passion centric or otherwise.

Passion Identity Tool

In order to provide guidance on the discovery of your passion, I have created a Passion Identity Tool. This tool is designed to break activities into 5 categories:

1) Non-negotiable activities - things that you have to do
2) Duty-based activities - things that you should do
3) Passion-based activities - things that fulfill you
4) Hobby-based activities - things that you like to do
5) Distractions - things that you do to pass time

Passion Identity Tool

Fire Your Job, Hire Your Passion

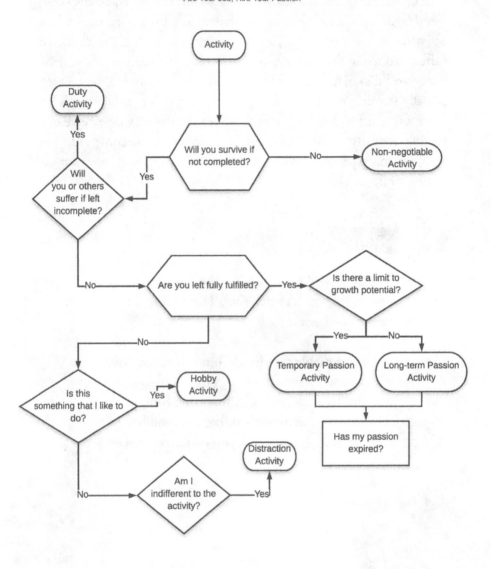

Let's take a look at each category in detail and see if we can start chipping away at your Passion Identity.

BILLY F. WROE JR.

Non-Negotiables

Regardless of the lifestyle we live, non-negotiable activities exist for all of us. These are the activities that keep us alive. Some of these activities are automated and require little effort on our part. Others require intentional action to be implemented. For instance, if we fail to consume food or do not drink water for a long enough period, our body's ability to remain active ceases. Similarly, if we disable our ability to breathe by submerging ourselves deep underwater, the end result will be death.

Non-negotiable activities are easy to identify because we need only ask one question to determine the relevance of the activity. "Will you survive if the activity is left incomplete?" If the answer is "No" then the activity is vital. During swim week, Navy Seals undergo intense water training. Many of the tasks are performed in high stress and oxygen deprived environments. One of the greatest risks to Seals during this week is drowning. In some cases drowning occurs as a result of a phenomenon called surface blackout. A surface blackout occurs when a person goes too long without air and upon their return to the surface, they blackout before they can consume enough air to keep themselves conscious. In their unconscious state, the body falls back below the surface of the water and pulls water into the lungs and without rescue aid, death is imminent. Procrastinating on non-negotiable activities can have deadly results, but not all activities are immediately identified as non-negotiable.

While hiking in Blue John Canyon, canyoneer Aaron Ralston found himself with his right arm trapped under a boulder. I imagine when Aaron initially asked himself would he survive if he just laid there trapped on day 1, there was not a definitive yes or no that he could attach to his actions. After lying pinned for 5 days, now with no food or water, Aaron found an absolute answer to his question and suddenly the action of lying trapped beneath the boulder became a life or death decision. As a result, Aaron used his pocketknife to amputate his right arm, freeing himself from the boulder and enabling him to move to a location where the search and rescue teams looking for him would have a better chance at finding him. Fortunately, because of Aaron's willingness to continue to ask himself the important non-negotiable question surrounding his situation, he was able to make the decision to endure excruciating pain in order to survive. Just because we ask ourselves the survivability question once does not mean that we should not ask ourselves the question again when necessary. While our answer is "Yes" or unknown, it is important to remember that we are not interacting with a non-negotiable activity at that moment (even when it feels like you are). In order to maintain potency, we should ensure that we put as few activities as possible into the non-negotiable category. There are always more questions that we can ask ourselves to determine what type of activity we might be interacting with.

Duties

If we determine that the activity does not meet the non-negotiable test criteria, then we move to the next important activity type, duty-based activities. Duty-based activities consist of activities that should be completed, but they are not critical to our survival. The question I use to determine if an activity fits into this category is "Will you or others suffer if the activity is left incomplete?" If the answer is "Yes" then you are likely interacting with a duty-based activity. For me, fatherhood is a very important duty-based activity. If I leave the task of being a father to my children incomplete, we both suffer. The children suffer from a lack of guidance and resources. I potentially suffer regret in the present and definitely in the future for not making an honest attempt to be the father that my children deserve. In order to avoid unnecessary suffering, fatherhood activities should be completed.

Sometimes we can attempt to force an activity into this category due to peer pressure or our own "self-righteous" (used loosely) desires. Yes, there is such a thing as faux duties. I have seen present parents unnecessarily bad mouth absent parents because they feel that it is their duty to inform the child about the inadequacies of the other parent. This often arises from a place of anger and frustration, but it also causes suffering for the child rather than relief. The true duty of the parent is their responsibility to guide the child to a healthy rendition of adulthood. That guidance does not require you to tear down the other parent. One might say that they and the child suffer from the other parent's absence, but that duty belongs to the absent parent not the present one. The present parent's responsibility is to provide contrast as to what the healthy example should look like. Only then are they truly meeting the obligations of their duty. Keep it simple, if you will not die, and no one will suffer then we are potentially interacting with one of my favorite activities, our passion. This is where the excitement comes in.

Passions

Unlike the first 2 categories in the Passion Identity Tool, our passions come with 2 questions. The first question is to help to determine if we are interacting with a passion in general. "Will you be left fulfilled?" When we interact with our passions, we are left with the complex feelings of fulfilment that I described in the beginning of the chapter. This does not mean that we don't desire additional interaction with the activity, but we find more than just a surface level of enjoyment out of our overall experience with it. Music is one of the activities that I am passionate about. It is not just listening to music, but writing my own melodies and lyrics, performing shows, and picking out new intricacies between the different instruments. Music brings me life! With the right type of music, I can be moved emotionally, mentally, and even spiritually. My passion for music provides a depth of comfort and surety that transcends my current state of circumstances. It is because of this response that I have to music that I know that music is one of my many passions. But the second question the Passion Identity Tool asks is designed to move from general passion to specific passion type.

- **Passion point:** Your passions do not have to be larger than life activities. Passions can be found in the simplicity of a flower or the rage of the sea.

Long-term and Short-term Passions

Long-term Passions

A passion can either be long-term or short-term. In order to help decide which type of passion I am engaged in, I have learned to ask the following question: "Is there a limit to my growth potential?" What I mean by growth potential is an assessment of my ability and willingness to continue learning new things as I engage with my passion. By asking this question, I am determining if my passion has the potential to become stagnant or stale. Let's go back to music. Is there a limit to music's growth potential as a passion? New music is created every day and even if new music was never created again, I could start listening to music in new languages to expand deeper into my musical passion. There is always an area available for me to grow and expand, thus it is highly probable that music is a long-term passion. However, all that glitters is not gold in the world of passion. Some growth opportunities can be misleading.

A while back I had a conversation with a friend that is heavily into fitness about whether she was going to compete in another body-building competition. When we first met, she had recently completed a local body-building competition and was still riding the high. To prepare for the competition, she invested hours in the gym working out and practicing poses. During that time, she was very passionate about staying connected to the competition community which in turn kept her connected to fitness. It appeared that she had found the next area of growth for her fitness passion, so I was shocked when she said that she was no longer interested in entering another competition. She realized that though she enjoyed everything that the process of competition provided her, it was more of a one time achievement than a lifestyle. She is still just as passionate about fitness, but trusts herself enough to know what applies to that passion. Just because we can or do expand into a new area of growth does not mean that the expansion is required to be maintained. It is important to trust your intuition on what feels right. Don't be afraid to take a step back and determine if the growth was a check off the bucket list, or even if a long-term passion has run its course.

Short-term Passions

On the opposite spectrum of our long-term passions are short-term ones. Both long and short timeframes are relative to the individual, so when I refer to short-term passions in this context, I am referring to passions that have a growth cap that can cause our feelings of fulfillment to quickly fade. Think about how excited you were when you first learned how to tie your shoes. I would dare say that for a moment in time, it was a passion. Every opportunity to show someone that you were able to tie your shoes was filled with so much pride. However, by the time you are about 10-years old, no one is moved by your ability to tie your shoes anymore, not even you.

With short-term passions it is a little easier to predict when the passion will fizzle out. By making an honest assessment of our level of interest and why we are interested, we can identify milestones that will be encompassed at the climax of our experience. These insights allow us to set clear expectations of the indicators that will signal that our passion is coming to an end. If the space for growth can be filled rapidly, then our passion will climax rapidly and our excitement begins to dull at an even faster rate than that which was built during its accent. This does not make short-term passions any less meaningful than long-term ones. Passion is passion, and as such, regardless of the duration, it can be susceptible to fatigue.

Passion Fatigue

As with clothes and relationships, it is possible to outgrow some passions. When we try to hold on to passions beyond their expiration date we experience passion fatigue. Passions are designed in a way that even when they drain us, they give something back to us in exchange. Farmers work for months in the field, but they also enjoy the fruits of their labors. Passion fatigue occurs when we experience an extended duration of significant energy output paired with little to no reward from the outcome of the expired passion. It is like having a bank account that you put money into every day, only to have that money spent on daily account fees, so you never gain any traction and your reserves never grow. In order to avoid passion fatigue it is important to accept when a passion has run its course, and just as spoiled food is still food, an expired passion is still a passion, it is just more likely to make you sick than nourish you.

Hobbies

As much as I am fulfilled by my passion for writing, I can't picture myself doing it all day, every day. I also like to workout, play basketball, video games, and other activities that are not passions. If passions give our lives purpose, then hobbies are the texture of that purpose. Similarly to how a valley defines the height of a mountain, our hobbies measure the scope of our passions. Hobbies are the activities in life that we enjoy that do not meet the depth of fulfillment that our passions provide. To identify hobby activities, ask yourself, "Is this activity something that I like to do?" When the answer is yes, you are dealing with a hobby. The Passion Identity Tool intentionally asks questions about passion before exploring hobbies to help reduce confusion.

- **Passion point:** One person's passion can be another person's hobby and vice versa. Be careful not to adopt the emotions of others as your own for the activities that you engage in.

Hobbies are important because they keep our passions from completely consuming our life. They are the breaks we willfully engage in to mentally recharge between interacting with our passion. The result is the difference between trying to recharge your phone while using it versus charging the phone with the power off. There have been numerous times when I have been in the middle of writing and I have turned on a game to just take a break from the creation process required to write this book. The result is enough down time to alleviate the fatigue and stress that hours of writing can place on my mind. The part of my brain that I use for solving video game problems is completely different from the effort it takes to overcome writing challenges.

Hobbies can also act as an incubation chamber for passions during their infancy. When I initially started writing poetry in junior high, it was just a hobby. I was not fulfilled by writing, I simply enjoyed it from time to time. I did not realize that those infrequent and inconsistent interactions were helping to hone my ability to articulate my thoughts into written words. Seven years later, as I started to outline my first concept for a book, my hobby began to gradually transition into the passion it is today. Today, my writings fulfill me and inspire me to continually grow through frequent engagement. Though I wish that our hobbies were the last category on the Passion Identity Tool, there is one more category that I am required to mention in order for the guidance to be complete.

Distractions

Once we move through all other activity options on the Passion Identity Tool, we arrive at the final category, distractions. Distractions are the activities that we engage with simply to pass time. The question I ask to reveal the subtle nature of these types of activities is: "Am I indifferent to the activity?" When we are not moved one way or the other by an activity its only purpose is to fill time with something, elsewise the time would simply be empty. Unfortunately, these activities are typically devoid of personal growth. Additionally, distractions interfere with other more meaningful activities.

Our distractions often appear in the form of unconscious habits. Have you ever awakened in the morning, grabbed your phone to turn off your alarm and an hour later realized that you are still in the bed scrolling through social media before your feet even hit the ground? What happened is that you have allowed social media (a distraction) to hijack the intent of the moment. You did not set an alarm to wake up and scroll down the timeline of someone's page or to watch their latest cat video. It is the same as if a plane were being flown by autopilot without a destination. The plane could maintain altitude by flying in circles for hours, but eventually it will run out of fuel. We have the same ability to fall into this non-destination-auto-pilot cycle, but rather than jet fuel we are burning time and energy. These types of distractions typically occur during our quiet time. However, distractions do not only exist in isolation.

When I was about 20 years old, there was a period in time when I caught public transportation for about a year. One day between transferring from the bus to the light rail I ran into an old high school friend. When we first saw each other we were both happy that our paths crossed as it had been about 3 years since we had connected. We sparked up a conversation to catch up and things quickly went downhill from there. After about his third sentence, I realized that none of the words being shared created a coherent thought. Fifteen minutes later, the light rail arrived and we departed. As the doors closed on the train, I remember feeling frustrated that I had wasted 15 minutes of my time listening to a person talking about nothing. I came to 2 realizations in that moment that I still carry with me to this day: 1) People can be distractions, and 2) Whenever possible, I would no longer allow someone to fill my time unnecessarily.

People can have the best intentions when interacting with you. As such, they can come from places of love, empathy, compassion, encouragement, and support. As wonderful as these perspectives are, we are the keepers of how we spend our time. Distractions with people can be difficult to identify. This is why doing a check on our indifference is so important. Take talking on the phone. Talking on the phone can be a distraction when talking to the wrong person or a passion when conversing with the right one. If we are talking just to talk because we have some free time available, but are not actively nurturing the relationships that we value, we are distracted. However, if we have time available to talk and are intentionally using that time to deepen our important connections, we are actually focused.

It is easy to get wrapped up in a distraction, but because the activity is unimportant it is equally easy if not easier to disengage from it. One tactic that I have used to interrupt distraction activities is a 5-second rule. Once I realize that I am doing an activity just to do something and that there is no real value being created, I give myself 5 seconds to intentionally shift from distraction to a more meaningful use of my time. I literally countdown and before I hit 0 I require myself to take action. This short exercise even helps me in the gym when I am tired and don't want to put in another set. It acts as a catalyst to focus my actions in order to shift away from distraction activities and towards more meaningful activities within the Passion Identity Tool.

Shifting categories

Every category in the Passion Identity Tool, other than non-negotiable activities, has the potential to shift. There are 2 goals that the tool is designed to help you achieve. The first goal is simply to help you avoid distractions. Distractions can cause us to miss multiple opportunities to engage with our passions and should be avoided to the best of our ability. The second goal takes a little more effort to achieve. Because the tool is designed to help us see our passions more clearly, it enables us to intentionally move aspects of those passions into duty-based activities. We will talk more about this in chapter 7 when we address developing your craft.

Let's go all the way back to the clucking duck. If an activity we are engaged with looks like our passion, but leaves us unfulfilled, we are interacting with a hobby. If we are only engaged because we have time to kill, we are interacting with a distraction, and should course correct as soon as possible. The identity of our passion is complex, and the more we are fulfilled by it today, the more likely we are to interact with it tomorrow. At times, we may feel that we will never know what our true passions are. Overall, we must remember to be patient with ourselves in gaining these insights and that this journey of discovery is not a sprint but a marathon.

Timeout: Passion Identity Tool Practice

*Grab your **Passion Journal**. Take a moment to review the Passion Identity Tool categories. Now, using the activity that you are currently engaged in (reading) let's determine how that corresponds to your passion identity. It is not about how what you are reading resonates with you, but the purpose of what the activity of reading is to you that matters. These are the questions I would like you to ask yourself about reading. Once you answer yes to one of the questions, stop and dig deeper.*

1. *If you do not read, will you die?*
    1. *Dig Deeper*
        1. *What will cause the death?*
    If you do not read, will you or others suffer as a result?
    1. *Dig Deeper*
        1. *What is the source of the suffering?*
        2. *Who suffers directly and/or indirectly?*
2. *Does reading fulfill you?*
    1. *Dig Deeper*
        1. *What emotions/feelings are encompassed in the complexity of fulfillment?*
        2. *Is there a limitation to the fulfillment?*

3. Is reading something that you like to do?
    1. _Dig Deeper_
        1. What enjoyment do you get from the activity?
4. Are you indifferent to reading?
    1. _Dig Deeper_
        1. Why do you choose this activity to preoccupy your time?
        2. Is there something else that you could do that would be more meaningful to you?

CHAPTER 6

Feel, Think, Passion

For the majority of my professional career, I have worked in environments that have stifled my desire to act based on emotion. Many times, I have opted to ignore the damage caused by these jobs by just chalking them up as a necessary evil of professionalism. In one aspect, this restraint was healthy because the actions I used in the tough neighborhood I grew up in were confrontational at best and destructive at their absolute worst. Typically I found myself falling somewhere between the 2 actions, leaning heavily in favor of destructive behaviors. On the opposite end of the spectrum, these environments allowed me to remain complacent in the area of improving my emotional intelligence (EQ). Though I was getting better at choosing less destructive (yet still confrontational) actions, my emotions or how to process them did not progress.

It was somewhere around my early 30s when I first stumbled across the world of EQ. Prior to delving into my emotions, I thought that I was ruled by logic. In fact, one of my favorite phrases was "Think then move." The challenge with this methodology is that biologically our brains are designed in such a way that we feel emotion in the limbic system of our brain prior to the information reaching the logic center found in the prefrontal lobe. In short, we are literally wired to feel before we have the opportunity to think. As a result, having a high intelligence quotient (IQ) can be bypassed when you have a low EQ.

For the purposes of this book, I will define emotional intelligence as one's ability to properly identify, manage, and process their emotional state in order to achieve healthy outcomes. EQ also involves being able to identify emotions in others, but we are going to focus our efforts on our own emotions. The debate on the number of core emotions that we have is somewhere between 4 and infinity. In order to not write a book within a book, we are going to limit our exploration into EQ to what I consider to be the 5 core emotions that we interact with as humans: happiness, sadness, fear, anger, and shame. Expanding your comprehension of these core emotions will help create a stronger EQ capable of developing deeper resilience within your passion.

The Emotional Hub

Emotions are one of the most powerful influences on how we make decisions. The Falling Man photo captured by Richard Drew is a reminder of just how powerful our emotions can be. Captured during the aftermath of the horrific tragedy of 9/11 after flight 175 hit the South Tower of the World Trade Center, an image of a man who appears to have jumped from the building captures him suspended in midair. There have to be intense emotions present in order to choose to jump from a building that high. There are countless stories like this, where emotion completely supersedes our logic.

During my previous experience working in the logistics industry, I learned quite a bit about the automated processes surrounding how packages move through a network. Regardless of what the package contains, at some point between picking it up from the customer and delivering it to the recipient, the package has to move through the hub. At the hub, there is a huge conveyor belt that the packages were placed on as they came off of large linehaul trucks. The purpose of the belt was to eliminate the need for drivers to have to walk back and forth to grab their packages by circulating them on a loop around the facility. Though there were thousands of packages daily, each driver had a station around the belt and was responsible for pulling the packages that correspond to their route.

Like with logistics, we all come equipped with an emotional hub. This place is where all of our emotions flow through towards their final destination, us. Unlike the drivers, who can cherry-pick only their packages, we do not get that same luxury when it comes to our emotions. How we initially feel about things is 100% automated. By accepting the fact that we are at the mercy of our emotions, we can avoid wasting our efforts to invalidate them. We cannot experience the emotion of sadness and decide not to feel sad at the same time. This is not to be confused with the actions that we take as a result of our emotions. Though those too may also feel 100% automated, I can assure you that is not the case. Since the emotional content that enters our life is outside of our control, the best thing we can do for our passion is implementing strategies that allow our emotions to support it. However, before we jump to strategy, we must first understand the role that the 5 core emotions play.

Emotional Support

Happy (Passion's Solar Power)

Though we may not experience it as often as we'd like, for many of us, happiness is our favorite emotion. To be in a happy emotional state is to be in a state of joy. We have all heard the phrase that time flies when you are having fun. Why is this statement universally accepted? The amount of unpleasant effort that we expend in an activity causes us to be more critically aware of the duration of time associated with the activity. When we are in a state of joy, not only does it make the moment feel effortless (which shifts our attention away from being critical about time to focusing more on the activity), it simply feels good. Think of it from a health perspective. If you were sick with the flu, you are probably lethargic and unmotivated to do small tasks or any task for that matter. Whereas when you are healthy and feel good, you could accomplish everything on your to-do list in a single day. When we are happy, an abundance of energy becomes available to execute our passion. In essence, our happiness can act as passion's solar power or renewable energy source, and the way we harness that energy is by creating joy around the processes involving our passion.

Sad (Passion's Compass)

If happiness is the fuel for our passion, sadness is the compass to it. To be sad is to be out of alignment with the outcome of our circumstances in a manner that leads to disappointment. Unlike a traditional compass that tells us where we are going, sadness is a compass that indicates that we are headed in the wrong direction. If you recall from chapter 5, our passion is designed to fulfill us. As an emotionally driven species, because sadness depletes us, our natural instinct is to attempt to move away from the source of that sadness. It is almost like being lost in the mountains. If we know that the town is at the bottom of the mountain and we are walking up towards the sky, it is clear that we need to turn around. Our passion heavily relies on our ability to interpret gloom in order to carve out the best path to achieving its objectives.

Fear (Passion's Ally/Adversary)

The human imagination never ceases to amaze me. Within my lifetime, we have gone from black-and-white televisions to autonomously driven vehicles. As wonderful as our imagination is, it is also a double-edged sword. F.E.A.R., or as I have referred to it for many years now, False Evidence Appearing Real, is our imagination's attempt to forecast the unknown. If you ask my sons, their dad is fearless, nothing scares me. However, if you ask me or anyone else for that matter, there are plenty of thoughts that can be absolutely horrifying. Fear is nothing more than an emotional story that taps into our primitive instinctual desire to survive. When something goes bump in the night, fear begins to narrate all of the potentially dangerous possibilities of what could be causing that noise. Fear can also manage social EQ scenarios that determine whether our attempts at finding belonging with peers will be accepted or rejected. When it comes to passion specifically, one thought that comes to mind is that we are inadequate to achieve success in our passion, and we will simply fail altogether. There are 2 things that we can do with this thought, and depending on which one we decide will determine if fear is an adversary or an ally.

When it comes to our passion, fear either exposes our cowardness or courage. What determines this is whether we are willing to either allow fear to bind us or prepare us. The moment we allow fear to imagine a story of failure that we adopt as inevitable, that fear becomes an adversary. Many times we are not even dealing with real-world opposition, but the thought that opposition could arise is significant enough for a lot of people to throw in the towel. In this case, fear binds us from pursuing progress in our passion.

- **Passion Point:** How many times have you allowed yourself to quit something that you are passionate about due to fear? How many more times are you going to allow this to be acceptable?

On the other spectrum of fear, the exact same story of failure can be imagined. However, when we adopt a stance that that failure can be overcome, fear becomes an ally. For instance, if we own a business and we are fearful that it may become insolvent, rather than closing up shop, we could save a little more cash to help keep the business afloat should hard times hit. By embracing fear as a healthy component of the pursuit of passion we can develop the courage necessary to forge ahead even in the face of expected or unexpected circumstances.

Anger (Passion's Enforcer)

If ever there were an emotional love story told about me, anger would absolutely be my #1 love interest. To be angry is to be upset with how we or another person has handled a situation. I have experienced intense anger towards myself when I felt that I could not only have done better making a decision, but the decision that I made was flat out stupid. I once had a person ask me if, because I have taken anger management classes, I no longer feel angry. I laughed as I responded and told them that the keyword was management, not annihilation. Whether regarding your passion or life in general, as you explore more of your emotions you will find that most of them are neutral. Emotion is neither good nor bad but serves a purpose. Anger can be used as fuel for our passion similarly to how nitro can temporarily boost a car's top speed, but unfortunately most of us (myself included) wield anger as a nuclear option and blow everything up.

Even as a temporary boost to something positive, anger can cause damage. In a passion excessively powered by anger, we can miss important steps, or we can cause damage to important relationships that anger tends to disregard. Anger is typically the enforcer we use to respond when we feel as if we have been attacked. Look at road rage incidents across America. One person cuts off another, and the action is received as an intentional act that warrants retaliation. What follows is a series of events in which both parties are willing to now risk their lives (and the lives of others on the road) to prove a point. Wielding nuclear anger can cause irreparable damage to our passion's impact, and a misunderstanding can quickly turn everything that you have built into a pile of rubble. Don't allow anger to be the foreman of your passion's demolition crew.

Shame (Passion's Borders)

Shame acts as the borders to which our passion is confined by society. When we cross these often superficial borders with our passion, we either quit, dial down our passion to get back inbounds, or choose to live outside of the norm. I recall being in elementary when I met Katie McFadden. Katie was a little girl who came to my school as a visitor from another school, to sing in our school's talent show. Her voice was beautiful and she most definitely had a passion for singing. However, not even a fourth of the way into her solo, the kids at my school began to heckle her to the point that she quit singing and ran off the stage crying. This is before the anti-bullying campaigns of today's generation. Shame is an emotion that measures our levels of embarrassment based upon social norms and at times unrealistic standards. Katie succumbed to the shame she felt in that performance, not because she was singing poorly, but because society (i.e. the mean kids at my school) was giving her feedback as if she were.

Shame is a deflating emotion that erodes our confidence, and as such can cause us to prematurely give up on our passion. Fortunately, Katie did not allow shame to end her passion for singing completely. Katie and I performed many more times around the state, and she still has a beautiful voice to this day. Rather than subscribing to the standards of how others felt about her singing, she chose to subscribe to her expectations which allowed her to continue to push into her passion for singing. This elementary lesson will not make you impervious to the impact of shame, but it can make sure that if you are going to adjust your passion based upon shame, at least be the party that sets the standard for yourself.

Whether happy, sad, fearful, angry, or ashamed, these 5 core emotions all play an important role in supporting the longevity of our passion. We never were intended to live an emotionless experience in this life. We were designed to feel our journey every step of the way. Now that we understand that we are at the mercy of our emotions and how our passion can benefit from those emotions, we can look at the next stage of developing our emotional intelligence. Our strategy.

No matter the ebbs and flows, emotions are something that we cannot escape. Vivian Green's R&B hit "Emotional Rollercoaster" shares this universal truth about emotions. Whether we are at our highest heights or other times our lowest lows, emotions are with us every step of the way. Many of us have attempted to sidestep this fact by developing coping mechanisms that ignore our emotional states. However, voluntary ignorance of our emotions can create larger issues than interacting with the emotion would. In her 2013 Ted Talk, Eleanor Longden shared vividly how her unwillingness to process the emotions she experienced during traumatic events in her life led to a diagnosis of schizophrenia. It wasn't until Eleanor identified the emotions that each voice represented and opened a dialogue with them that she was able to begin her healing process. Eleanor's experience may be a rare case, but it identifies the importance of moving beyond building coping mechanisms and to begin developing processing methods.

If the story of Troy taught us anything, it's that we cannot hide behind our walls forever. Eventually, something sneaks through, and we either deal with it or it destroys us. Coping mechanisms are the walls in which we hide behind during the early developmental stages of our EQ. They act as training wheels, temporary in nature, allowing us to stabilize the unfamiliar by finding our emotional balance point. Think about a child that brings a security blanket to the first day of preschool as a temporary confidence boost, the blanket acts as a shield from what can be a slightly overwhelming emotional experience. Now imagine that same security blanket is brought to the first day of work as an adult. One might think that the adult may have relied upon that blanket well beyond its expiration date. Investing in a long-term coping mechanism strategy cripples our ability to handle emotions when they sneak past our defenses. The security blanket was not designed to increase confidence, it was only made to create a space to build upon the emotions that support confidence. It is only when we put ourselves out there to experience both rejection and acceptance that the need for the blanket begins to dissolve. However, we are not out of the woods yet.

Let's say that the average restaurant serves about 30 customers per hour and is open for 10 hours a day, 7 days per week. If each customer orders one meal from the menu that is 300 meals served each day. What do you think would happen if the restaurant saved all of their orders until the end of the day and then began cooking them? The kitchen would be a madhouse. You could easily run out of plates, utensils, staff, or your primary product, food. Now multiply those 300 meals by a week (2,100 meals), a month (9,000 meals), or even a year (109,500 meals) and the story quickly spirals out of control. In order for the restaurant to remain in business, they have to develop a process that allows meals to flow through as they are ordered. Our emotions operate in a similar manner. The average adult feels approximately 3 to 4 emotional events daily. Unfortunately, unlike meals in a restaurant, there is no set menu as to which emotions will arise on any given day. Our passions cannot function at their peak performance if these emotional events backlog and wreak havoc on our EQ. In order to maintain a high EQ, much like the restaurant, our emotions must be processed as the demand arises.

Processing emotions is the natural progression as we move away from coping mechanisms. There is only one way to process your emotions, and that is to interact with them no matter what they feel like. The sooner we interact with our emotions, the better it is for our EQ. However, one of the most difficult things for me to learn in my adolescence of EQ was that most of the interaction with emotion required inward reflection and not outward expression.

Timeout: Emotional Check-in

*Grab your **Passion Journal**. Take a moment to replay your day. What emotional events have you felt thus far? Did you gloss over the events or did you stop to engage with them? If you chose to engage with your emotions, did you do so in a healthy manner?*

Resistance, Interpretation, & Motion (R.I.M.)

When we process our emotions as they occur, we help our brain build faster connections between the limbic system (emotional center) and the prefrontal cortex (logic center). The more connections we are able to establish, the faster information moves between the 2 regions. Unfortunately, the number of fibers sending information from the limbic system to the prefrontal cortex is greater than what is coming in from the prefrontal cortex. This is why sometimes we experience overwhelmingly intense emotions that make it feel almost impossible to create a clear thought. EQ, or the lack thereof, is one of the key reasons that many people abandon their passions. As such, it is of the utmost importance that we learn how to engage with our emotions in real-time. In order to help you achieve this goal, I have created a simple 3-step method that has helped me to create favorable outcomes when feeling overrun by emotions. Resistance, Interpretation, & Motion (R.I.M.)

Resistance

To be completely honest with you, I created the R.I.M. processing method out of sheer necessity. After decades of overreacting to my emotions, I finally arrived in a place where I realized that my emotional outbursts were leading me down a path filled with destruction. I allowed my emotions, especially ones that I reacted to negatively, to surprise me even when I knew they were on the horizon. This is where I found that step 1 in the R.I.M. process came into focus. The R in R.I.M. represents Resistance. Fortunately prior to defining the R.I.M. process, my interaction with emotions originated from a place of resistance. Unfortunately, I resisted allowing myself to experience my emotions through the use of an emotion suppression coping mechanism. I'll admit, it was a horrible attempt to become an emotionless Volcan from the sci-fi series Star Trek. Like many people, I associated feeling emotions that I reacted to negatively with the destructive behaviors that followed them, so of course, the solution was to become numb to my experiences. As I began to develop the R.I.M. process, I quickly learned that my destructive actions were the issue and not my emotions themselves. As such, I trained myself to shift my efforts away from the emotion avoidance behaviors, to focusing on resisting the urge to take immediate action.

Giving yourself time to feel an emotion and not allowing yourself to jump into immediate action helps the mind's ability to process what it is experiencing. Rather than your mental capacity being inundated by the actions that your body has physically taken in response to its emotionally compromised state, you free up bandwidth which creates intentional EQ space for resolution. Through the proper use of resistance, I learned that the only urgency for action was to be still and feel the emotion. This can be experienced over a matter of seconds or over a matter of months. The time for resistance may vary, but the important thing to learn is that hesitation can be your greatest ally along the path to understanding and fully processing your emotions. By taking a moment to resist our emotional impulses, we help to create a stronger foundation for the second stage in the R.I.M. process to be established upon.

Interpretation

For a moment, think of your emotions as you would a foreign language. Yes, you can hear the words of a foreign language, but because you don't have a point of reference to associate with the words, you are unable to comprehend them. It is only after you study the language that you become capable of understanding the words. Foreign emotions operate in the same manner. In the Interpretation stage of the R.I.M. method, we begin to ask important questions as a means of research in an effort to gain critical insight into our emotions. Remember, there are hundreds of connections for sending emotions out, but far less for sending logic in. It is the equivalent of living in a city where there are a hundred lanes leading out of the city (limbic system), but only 2 lanes leading back into the city. You are bound to have traffic jams as information returns. In the

Interpretation stage, we begin to build new roads leading from the prefrontal cortex to the limbic system. These roads are built by asking ourselves the following questions:

- What emotion do I feel? (Identify)
- What does that emotion mean? (Hypothesize)
- Why do I feel that emotion right now? (Situational Awareness)

Do not be fooled by the appearance of simplicity that these questions present on the surface. I promised that they are loaded and at times you will struggle to even answer 1 of them. The purpose of these questions is to identify the emotion, hypothesize its meaning, and build situational awareness in regard to the application of that emotion. If the answers to the 3 questions do not align, then you may not have properly identified the emotion, or in some cases, you could be interacting with a default emotion which is corrupting the emotion of the experience altogether.

Default Emotions

Default emotions are the emotions that we are most comfortable with and are heavily relied upon when we experience emotions that we are less familiar with. They act as an emergency lane to bypass the traffic leading back into the city. Have you ever found yourself in a set of circumstances where you thought you should feel one way, but felt totally opposite? Or maybe you have reflected on a moment when you did not react accordingly to a situation? Even if we obtain a high EQ, we all have default emotions. If you were to guess the default emotion for most Americans, what would you think it was? If you guessed anger, you guessed right. I wish I could say that I was unlike most Americans in this regard, but that would be false. From road rage to grocery store shouting matches, anger is often the emotion we lean on to resolve negative experiences.

- **Passion Point:** What is the default emotion that you tend to rely on more than others?

I once was in a situation where it took me days of asking the same interpretation questions because I kept identifying anger as the emotion that I felt. However, anger did not align with the situation I was involved in. Though I felt angry about the circumstances, when I finally uncovered the root of the experience, I found that I was actually hurt by the unforeseen scenario. Once I ran the emotion of hurt through the scenario, it allowed me to process the emotion in such a way that the conversations that followed did not require retaliation or a full-scale assault. Once we are able to identify and interpret an emotion, we are primed for the final stage on the R.I.M. processing method, Motion.

Motion

The first 2 stages of the R.I.M. processing method required stillness and reflection. In the motion phase, we now have enough information to take action and begin moving through the emotion itself. Moving through emotion can require either action, inaction, or a blend of both. Remember, the purpose of improving our EQ is to achieve healthier outcomes. The purpose of the movement phase is to determine what we want to do with the emotional information that we gathered in stages 1 and 2. For instance, if we are happy, how do we continue in that emotion? If we are angry, do we allow ourselves to lash out emotionally, or attempt to lend grace and understanding to the situation to respond appropriately? This phase is where many people experience the challenge involved with expanding their EQ because they do not want to deal with the discomfort of addressing their identified emotions.

In order to effectively move through emotion, it is important to know who you want to be. Our desired identity acts as a barometer for whether the actions we take will be deemed appropriate in order to complete the resolution process. This works well when we already have an established identity, but the real work is found in attempting to strive for an identity that we have yet to achieve. Regardless of which identity we choose, it is important that it originates from an authentic place. If our identity is heavily reliant upon what we believe to be social identity or who we want the world to think of us as egotistically, the motion phase will eventually fail and the backlog of emotional buildup will quickly overwhelm our efforts as all the unresolved emotions come flooding back to the surface. An example is a person who chooses an identity that spends money during the motion phase, they could be leaning on their financial coping mechanisms, and the moment they lack the financial ability to compensate for doing the real work, moving through the emotion, they will find themselves right back at square one in their EQ education.

There is no shortcut to moving through our emotions. The only way to develop a healthy processing method is to work through the process and not around it. There will be a tremendous amount of temptation to sidestep the emotional information that we gathered in stages 1 and 2, but I encourage you to continue to push forward. By doing so you not only become better acquainted with your own emotional triggers, but you will also begin to understand the type of responses that you desire for your emotions to drive.

The R.I.M. tool does not make emotions go away or magically become less difficult to address. It is a tool, and like all tools, when used properly it will assist you in keeping your commitment to the time and effort required to genuinely improve your EQ for both your sake and the sake of your passion. It is hard work, but I promise that the journey to gain emotional intelligence is worth the reward on the other side. By taking these 3 steps, resisting the urge to take immediate action, interrupting the emotional information, and then moving through the emotion, you will be well on the road to hiring your passion. Remember to feel before you think, think before you act, and always act according to who you authentically want to be.

CHAPTER 7

Developing Your Passion

One of my favorite speakers said, "Never work harder on your job than you are willing to work on yourself." At the end of the day, when you leave a job, you can only take you with you, not the job. It is interesting how many hoops we are willing to jump through to secure, keep, or promote into a "good-paying" job, while at the same time treating our passion as if it is an unworthy endeavor. We have subscribed to the logic that life is about either/or, and can never be a balance or intertwining of both, but that is not always the case. This is especially not the case when it comes to our passion. The truth is, that which we nurture in life thrives. The goal is to become so good at your passion that people are willing to pay you for it. It does not mean that you are obligated to monetize your passion, but look at it like this. How high of a level would you have to execute at for people to be willing to compensate you for your passion?

Whether we want to fire our job metaphorically or literally, we are going to have to figure out a way to increase our passion's value. A business mentor of mine would always remind me that people become successful overnight, just not last night. What he meant by this is that, there are many pieces to success that cannot be seen from a distance. Our ignorance to the hours filled with sweat, frustration, pain, tears, and failures can cause us to believe that what we are experiencing as we forge ahead with our own passion is the equivalent of running in quicksand. What many of us fail to acknowledge in these moments is that our journey is not theirs. The only universal component of our process is our passion's need for development.

Development is nothing more than the intentional improvement of a present state. If what we are capable of with our passion today is inadequate to achieve the goals that we have set for it, then it is our responsibility to demand more of ourselves. Since there is no shortage of books, YouTube tutorials, mentors, or programs designed to help us develop the skills that our passions are reliant upon, what keeps us from engaging with these things? The answer is simple: we do. Rather than doing the research to grow, many of us are heavily reliant upon the lessons derived solely from trial and error. Often, we look at trial and error as an opportunity to immediately jump into the action phase of our passion (undoubtedly the most exciting phase), and because we don't expend time and energy reading books, listening to lectures and taking notes, it feels more productive. However, before we explore trial and error, we must first have a clear understanding of the difference between *feeling* productive and *being* productive.

Optimal Productivity

Genuine productivity rarely comes at the expense of efficiency. I remember being assigned a project within my first 2 years as an analyst where my boss asked me to create regional reports for 23 regions. The reports were pretty straightforward, but they involved about an hour of data entry per region, so we were looking at 23 man hours each time we wanted to perform this level of detailed analysis. The insights that the reports would provide to our department and the operational teams was worth the investment. I remember sitting in my office as I worked on the first region. When it came time to manually enter the data, I thought to myself that I could probably write some code to automate parts of the process. The innovative delay had begun.

About 2 hours into writing code my boss called to ask which region I was working on, to his disappointment I was still on the first region. I attempted to explain that I was working to make the process faster, but my boss quickly got off the phone. Another hour passed, and the phone rang again for an update. Yup, I was still in the same region, validating that my code was performing as intended. This time, my boss voiced his frustration and said that we could not work 3 hours in a single region, or the project would never be completed. Again, I attempted to explain that I was working on automating the data entry process, but my boss quickly cut me off and told me that he would begin working on the next region, and to email him every time I completed a region. Three emails and 15 minutes later, I had completed 3 regions, it was at this point that my phone rang again.

My boss wanted to know how the first region took over 3 hours, and now I was completing the reports in 5 minutes. He was so curious that he called me into his office. When I came into the office he showed me how he was performing the data entry task. He had printed out the data for an entire region, placed a ruler on the paper to ensure that he was entering the right data points for each line, and he would use the 10-key pad to enter the data. It was a sound system for entering the information into the report template, and over 23 hours would accomplish the objective of the project. Then he asked me to show him my process. I exported the same data from the region to an Excel file, opened it, ran my macro, and 5 minutes later the entire report was complete. I told my boss that I understood that the first report took 3 hours, but I also understood that by investing the time upfront, I could cut a significant portion of the man hours out of the entire project. I was agitated that he would even question my work ethic. I told him, I could have simply felt productive by completing a region each hour, and he would have felt good about those results. However, in choosing efficiency I created optimal productivity which expedited my results and ensured that there were no errors that a manual process could produce. He had no choice but to agree and 3 months later, the process was a highlight of our department's contribution during an onsite visit by the president of the company.

When we sacrifice efficiency for productivity we make more work for ourselves than is actually required. We see this all the time with people who are so busy being busy, that they never accomplish anything. To obtain optimal productivity we must begin to measure productivity holistically. By looking at both our process and the potential improvements that we can make to it, we can determine if the juice is worth the squeeze. In other words, while it was logical to spend 3 hours on one report to save 55 minutes on each subsequent report, it does not make sense to explore a potential efficiency for 1 hour to save 2 minutes on a 20-minute project? Regardless of how we feel about it, in this case, simply doing the process would be optimal. As this relates to the development of our passion, by asking ourselves a series of intelligent questions, we can determine if we want its development to look and feel productive or do we want it to *be* productive. Once we have a clearer understanding of that decision, we can then begin to unpack trial and error.

Scientific Development (Trial and Error)

Trial and error in and of itself is not the enemy to the development of our passions. Actually it comes with 1 of 2 specific outcomes: we either succeed or we fail. Scientists use trial and error in their experiments all the time, and through numerous renditions they are able to solve some of the most complex problems known to mankind. Then shouldn't trial and error alone work to develop our passions? It does when we take a scientific approach. Scientists do not aimlessly perform experiments. They undergo years of education, studying, and attending lectures long before they sit in a lab to attempt to solve problems as critical as Covid-19 vaccines. The key to their success is found in the intentionality behind their development.

Whether or not we choose to monetize our passions, we have to learn how to be focused on intentional development. You don't have to be an expert to begin the monetization process, but you also cannot be completely ignorant either. Some people live their passions on paper for their entire lives paralyzed by the fear that they don't know enough to be of value to others. Other people adopt the fake-it-until-you-make methodology, building upon hollow values in the absence of actual value. What we are looking for is a goldilocks zone. This is the place where our passion has some substance, but also has plenty of room for growth. In this space we not only use our research prior to taking action, but we also take notes on the process. And just as scientists use their notes to duplicate their successes and avoid repeating failures, we will do the same as we develop our passions.

Every math class that I have ever taken has always had one rule: show your work. By showing your work, you can typically go back through an incorrect answer and find the error in the calculation. Being a person who can do math in my head relatively well, I used to hate this rule. However, as a coach and author, I cannot express enough the importance of taking notes. Because I am inundated with an abundance of thoughts daily, I have learned that when I have a thought worth remembering it is important to send myself a text to capture it before it escapes. In the same manner that this gives me the opportunity to revisit an idea at a later time, taking notes on how we are developing our passion allows us to revisit our takeaways from our experiences. If you recall the time machine we used in chapter 1 to revisit the past and future, notes act in a similar manner, but with the advantage of placing the experience in slow motion for deeper review. I know, this sounds like a lot of work that we don't have time for, but I promise, no matter what you have going on in your life, you have the time. As we move through this chapter, begin to think about how you can nurture your passion daily. What are the intentional moments that you can create, and the stolen moments that you can repurpose?

One of the challenges of being an adult is that we spend so many years prior to and into adulthood living life based upon schedules that are provided to us by others. When you are a baby, your parents try to put you on sleeping and feeding schedules. As you reach adolescence you have school, chores, bedtimes, and other schedules that are thrust upon you. Finally as an adult the schedule above all schedules, the work schedule comes into play. The fact that these schedules are provided for us for decades typically weakens our ability to prioritize activities. I use a 3-phase process with my clients to help them overcome this scheduling atrophy and identify available time to develop their passions.

The success schedule tool uses a simple tracking spreadsheet to break down the entire week hour by hour, 24 hours a day. In the first phase (about a 2 week period) it allows the user to document each hour of their current routine. Each item has a category that it falls into: sleeping, eating/cooking, working, grooming, family time, personal development, social media time, phone time, etc. At the end of each day the number of hours spent in each category are tallied and should equal 24 hours. During this period, I have often found that my client's schedules are on autopilot and they are just passengers to their own existence. Yes, there are responsibilities that must be attended to, but it is the time in between those responsibilities which lack guidance.

The second phase of the success schedule process (typically 4 weeks) is probably the most tedious. In this phase, we are asked to write out the number of hours we want to allocate to each category daily. This number does not have to be uniform. Each day is treated individually and can consist of whatever the desire is for that specific day. For instance, maybe Monday, Tuesday, Thursday, and Friday you want to sleep 6 hours, but on Wednesday, Saturday, and Sunday you want to sleep 7 hours. Once we have the desired hours allocated, we look at the variance between that and the prior 2 success schedules. This allows us to visualize how far off we are from where we want to be. We then take the responsibilities that cannot be moved, such as work, and plug them into the calendar for the upcoming week. Thus begins the negotiation of priorities.

In essence, the success schedule only has room for 24 items a day. If you work an 8-hour day, 5 days a week, that means that outside of your commute time, you have 5 days where you are left with only 16 items including sleep. Granted, not all activities are exactly an hour, but the reason I use 1 hour increments in the success schedule is to create leftover time when things finish early. Once the week starts, we use a blank success schedule to fill out what is actually done throughout the day, and the pre-planned schedule as a guide and to capture when things end early or run over. At the end of each day a comparison between the actual activities and the planned activities is reflected upon to determine what caused the plan to veer off course. In addition, by using the actual schedule we are able to determine the cumulative amount of time available from all events that ended early.

By analyzing deviations from the plan, we are able to identify time traps. Did we spend too much time on social media? Did we sabotage our day by hitting the snooze button 5 too many times? Did not meal prepping lunch the prior day impact our lunch plans today? Whatever the reason, don't be too hard on yourself, as many of us are novices in this area. Remember that the purpose of the exercise is to improve, not beat yourself up. On the other side of the coin, how much additional leftover time was available to you? This is where the magic of the success schedule begins to surface. In my primary checking account all transactions are rounded up to the nearest dollar and the difference between the purchase and the next dollar are transferred directly into my savings. Transferring $0.35 to savings may not seem like a lot, but over time, the amounts have totaled up to a couple hundred dollars. Having 30 - 45 minutes extra a day may not sound like a lot of time, but 3.5 - 5.25 hours a week is like having a part-time day to work on developing your passion. Not all of the time has to be dedicated to development either, it can also be allocated to rest, relaxation or other activities. The choice is yours.

The third phase of the success schedule process is ongoing. Not in the sense of forever, but until we develop a new autopilot program that achieves the better results that we seek, we will have to repeat this exercise weekly. In this phase we write out our success schedule, predetermine what we are going to do with our leftover time, and outside of an emergency, we stick to the plan. It really is no different from a work schedule. We arrive at our scheduled time for work, put in our hours, and go home when we are done. We are just taking this same mindset and applying it to our entire day. Though using these steps will help make space to develop your passion, you will still need to find the inspiration to take advantage of it.

Intrinsic Value

Our passion has both an external value (the value that others place on our passion) and an intrinsic value (the value that we assign to our passion). We will talk more about external value in chapter 9, but for now let's focus on intrinsic value. To consistently expend the energy necessary to develop our passion, we must first increase its intrinsic value to ourselves. Though the increase happens gradually over time, the first step to finding the inspiration necessary is acceptance. This means that no matter what our particular passion is, we have to accept that there is a market that we can tap into that is willing to pay for it. Even if that initial market is only us. Compensation is not always about man-made currency. When we are the market for our passion, the currency that we spend on it is our time. Our passion's intrinsic value is largely influenced by how we perceive our passion altogether. When we devalue our passion, we interpret efforts associated with improving our skills as costing too much or as a waste of time. On the other hand, when we value our passion, those exact same efforts can be associated with investing in order to achieve a good return on investment.

- **Passion Point:** If you had to spend $1,000 to improve one of your passions, how would you feel about it?

If I were to tell you that you have 24 hours to come up with as many hundred dollar bills as you can, and at the end of that time-frame I guaranteed you $2,000 for every $100 bill you accumulated, how hard would you work to accumulate as many bills as possible? I can tell you, I would not sleep for 24 hours. This is the mentality that we must work to embrace when it comes to valuing our passion. Inspirational speaker Brian Tracy once did a talk on how we could increase our income by 100 times. At the time I was making $40k a year and thought that it was fairytale thinking. This is because my value was attached to employment. I was not a professional sports athlete, doctor, lawyer, or actor, so how was I supposed to make $400k (10 times) in a year, let alone $4 million (100 times)? As an employee it would be impossible, but by choosing to employ our passion, the opportunities to achieve such a feat increase exponentially.

Once we have accepted our passion's value, to continue to increase our intrinsic value we must determine why our passion resonates with us and expand upon that focus. As a child, around the age of 12, John Moschitta began working on his passion for talking fast. His original reason was to break a Guinness record and have $2,000 donated to cerebral palsy research. It would be years before John was entered into the Guinness record as the fastest talking man, but while he worked towards his goal he gained other indirect benefits. It turns out sitting in his room for hours on end reciting tongue twisters to condition his mind and mouth to move at an almost inhuman speed, also increased his reading speed. If you were a child in the 80s, you may remember John by his nickname, "The Micro Machines Guy," and up until 2013, the holder of the Guinness World Record for the fastest talking man. John read the Micro Machines' commercials from a teleprompter which meant that if he could read a Micro Machines commercial, he could also read Minute-Rice, FedEx, and other commercials. Today John's net worth is around $3 million, a return well above his initial goal to donate $2,000.

Understanding what our investment of time, energy, and resources means to the future of our passion determines how we will develop that passion over the years. As we increase our intrinsic value, we will be inspired to put forth the effort to develop our passion in a way that is optimally productive and duplicatable, ensuring that as opportunities arise for our passion to make an impact we are at the ready. The value of my passion for helping to develop people based upon my experiences is that I extend my ability to be a person actively working to change the world for the better. Changing the world is important to me because my loved ones and I live in it. Know that at the end of the day, a valuable passion will drive you to hustle rather than settle for complacency. Whether or not you choose to monetize that passion is completely up to you. However, always keep in mind: it is not the money that drives the development of our passion, but it is the development that increases our passion's value. Ideally passion should fluctuate between learning and action phases based upon the demands of the situation. Who knows, the next investment towards growth could be your hundred-fold return.

CHAPTER 8

Adjusting Your Frequency

I grew up in an era when the television was so big that it was a standalone piece of furniture that sat on the floor. We were very much a play-outside generation of children, but come Saturday morning, almost every house in America with a child in it was tuned into Saturday morning cartoons. After a bowl of cereal, hours were spent laughing, performing makeshift karate moves, and learning important character lessons as 30-minute shows came into the house across the airwaves. If you counted the ones with static, there were about 50 channels to choose from, but the only frequencies I was interested in were the cartoons.

What is amazing about this moment of my childhood as I reflect upon it as an adult, is the technology behind the experience. Broadcasting stations would send out analog signals that were received by an antenna attached to the house. The TV also had its own antenna (rabbit ears) that some people thought if they added aluminum foil to, they would see the clearest standard definition picture possible. However, once the TV was tuned to the station that you wanted to watch, you were able to view the programming.

What if I told you that our passion has a frequency that it operates on? How we tune into that frequency is a lot like adjusting the antennas on the old TVs. Rather than using aluminum rabbit ears to view the programming, we simply adjust ourselves. I am not talking about some contorted yoga pose that one must master, but actually reprogramming our minds. Quite a few years ago, while meditating, I arrived at an amazing truth, that all things are being broadcast throughout the entire universe at all times to everyone. Sit with that for a moment. This means that the iconic iPhone has always been available to exist. The materials to build the phone and the electromagnetic waves for a phone signal were always present. The iPhone was just waiting for the right person (anybody) to understand how to create it. If you don't believe me, answer this question. Did fire exist before we gained the understanding on how to create it on our own and use it as a tool? It is not our knowledge that brings these things into existence, but our understanding of it that allows us to manifest them in the present. If this is the case with technology and nature, why would our passion be any different? Greatness, mediocrity, love, depression, wisdom, passion, everything is being transmitted waiting for those who are willing to tap into the signal.

The Law of Attraction & Work

If you have ever read the book *The Secret* by Rhonda Bryne, the law of attraction is not a new concept to you. If you have not, the law of attraction states that which you focus your thoughts upon will be attracted to you. If we focus on bills, more bills will come. If we focus on income, more money will come. If we focus on a specific type of relationship, more of those relationships will come. And, if we focus on our passion, we will attract more of it into our lives. Sounds a lot like a no diet, no exercise weight-loss program, right? I can assure you that this is far from an effortless endeavor.

I have told my oldest son numerous times that he could have anything that he wanted in life, as long as he was willing to do the work. The law of attraction is not any different. I have heard many people say that the law of attraction did not work for them. They thought about money, and bills came. They focused on love, but only found empty relationships. The common thread with these people was one thing. Whenever I asked them what they did to attract what they wanted outside of thinking about it, nothing else was added to the process. It's like putting a tea bag in a cup without water and expecting a cup of tea. The law of attraction is not only a law of wants, wishes, and desires. Focusing your thoughts only initiates the process, but is not enough energy to see it through to fruition. If real energy is not flowing into what we are saying that we are focused on, then our attention is actually elsewhere. More so, if we don't like the results that we are attracting, our focus needs to be refined. That is work that we are responsible for, and only we can complete it for ourselves.

The law of attraction is designed in such a way that it places the work required to receive that which we seek to attract in the forefront of our mind. Think of it like expecting a baby. You have fewer than 9 months to prepare the things that you need before the baby arrives. You spend time preparing for the arrival of the baby because you believe it is going to arrive. Somewhere along the way you may find out the baby's sex and start to buy the things that you think that you would need. You don't simply believe and hope that a crib shows up and puts itself together without any effort on your part. I am currently using the law of attraction to write this book. When I started, I did not know every word that I would write, or even the message in its entirety. All I knew is that I wanted to write a book that would have a profound impact on the lives of those who decided to read it. The desire to attract such a book has required me to dedicate energy to understanding its creation. There have been days where I have awakened at 3 in the morning with ideas that never would have come to me if I was not in this process. I have dedicated entire weekends to the process, because I believe at the end, I will receive a life-changing book, not only for the readers, but also for myself. It doesn't mean that I always want to do the work, but the small deposits of energy over time have a compounding effect that creates the effortless feelings that some experience with the law of attraction. In essence, the subtle habits that we form during preparation diminishes our ability to perceive the work we actually do, and before we know it, our thoughts become reality.

Timeout: What are you attracting?

*Grab your **Passion Journal**. Take the next 60 seconds to think about one thing that you recently attracted to yourself. Take the first thing that comes to mind, no matter how big or small it is. Now use the next 5 minutes to write down how you know that you attracted this to your life. Where were your thoughts? What actions led to its manifestation? Was the outcome positive or negative? Once you finish answering these questions, decide whether you want to attract more or less of this outcome in your life. What is one thing you can do in the next moment to increase or decrease the signal that you are receiving? Later when you have about 30 minutes do this same exercise again only using one of your passions as the attraction subject. Remember, there is an abundant signal waiting for you to tap into it.*

Our Personal Broadcast (A Two-Way Signal)

On June 12, 2009, all of those Saturday morning cartoon signals that were being broadcast over analog frequencies ceased, as the Federal Communications Commission's mandatory digital broadcasting signal regulations went into effect. This caused those who did not have a digital converter for their TV to no longer be able to receive programming with their analog antenna. The other part of the law of attraction that is frequently overlooked is that it is a two-way signal. We are not only constantly receiving information, but we are also broadcasting it as well. The result of our personal broadcast is that we build resonance with other people operating at similar frequencies and dissonance with those who are not. This is crucial to understand because signals are in a constant state of fluctuation, so who we resonate with today may not be who we resonate with always. As our personal broadcast fluctuates, people fall into 1 of 3 categories: they either align, adjust, or unsubscribe to our signal altogether.

Alignment

Some of the people we know are just naturally in alignment with our personal broadcast. Have you ever met someone and immediately thought that they belonged to your tribe? These are the relationships that seem to have an eternal bond no matter where life takes us. We should foster these relationships as they are the ones that will help us stay focused on where our energy flows and push us to amplify our passion. When there is interference with our signal, these people call it out and hold us accountable. They are not in your corner to tell you yes all the time, but the feedback that they share about your personal broadcast always originates from a place of encouragement. It would take a massive event to alter the closeness and vulnerability of this relationship because it provides a perpetual synergy that continually rejuvenates both parties. You want as many of these types of people in your tribe as you can find, or that can find you.

Adjustment

As your personal broadcast fluctuates, there will also be people who attempt to adjust their signal to match yours. With these people, it is important that you trust your intuition. That gut feeling we have about people is revealed as our antenna picks up their personal broadcast in spite of what they present on the surface. There are some babies who have separation challenges, but when a baby that goes to almost anyone all of a sudden refuses to go to a specific person, it is the purest form of intuition. A baby does not know how to give the benefit of the doubt, or second guess what they are sensing. They only know that something is not right and they don't want it. We are all born with this sixth sense, but some choose to nurture it more than others. The end result is that they are faster at determining the intent of the broadcast and which of 2 types of people they are dealing with.

Users

The first type of person in this category are the people that we need to protect ourselves from. They are the people who adapt to our broadcast for the sake of what they can take from it. Access to parties, our network, and other resources is their primary objective. Once we are all used up, they are off to suck the energy out of the next opportunity. Comedian Ryan Davis had a post for a personal assistant. One of the requirements of the job was that the person could not be interested in seeking fame. Ryan understands that if fame is the goal of the person in this position, they could be willing to do anything to achieve it; including sacrificing all that he has worked to build. These people are actually disruptors and opponents of our vision, and would often rather see us fail than to succeed without them. One of the glaring characteristics about this type of person is that they tend to unnecessarily name drop famous people that are not relevant to the conversation. It is more so about who they know rather than what they know and understand. We honestly have enough of our own insecurities to deal with to be worried about those that want to drain us without helping to replenish that which they have used. Do your passion a favor and disconnect from these people immediately as their envy can have a devastating impact.

Growers

The second type of person in this category are the ones who have a true desire to grow, but they are still working to fine tune their broadcast. People grow at different paces, and that is ok. The important thing is that they are open to growth in general. Though these people will take energy from your passion, each time they reach a new level of growth, that energy will be replaced with a little extra. Your role with people who are growing is as a mentor. Not in the sense of enforcing rules, but by teaching them how to reach their next level, you will boost their signal in such a way that their confidence is capable of maintaining that signal on its own. Characteristically, growers tend to have a strong sense of gratitude for the ones who are assisting them. In my experience as a developer of growers, I have always gained new insights from the lessons that I taught. Over time these relationships help us obtain John C. Maxwell's fifth level of leadership, Established Leadership.

Unsubscribers

The third and final category of the recipients of our personal broadcast is unsubscribers. These are the ones that have no interest in our frequency whatsoever. This is not always a permanent state, but it is an area that we should allocate zero energy to. Sometimes, people from other categories abruptly shift into this one. Unfortunately, when the relationship has been in place for a significant period of time and this occurs, we often try to fight to maintain the connection. Because the other party has no desire to tune into our personal frequency, any attempt that we make to attempt to sell them on its merit will inevitably fall flat. It is like a butterfly coming back to lecture a caterpillar who is complaining about how the butterfly has changed. The metamorphosis process between the two is so significant that a caterpillar cannot comprehend the change that they themselves may undergo, because the two no longer speak the same language.

Unsubscribers can also be difficult to let go when we allow our ego to get in the way. What happens is, rather than sending an authentic broadcast our goal becomes showing the uninterested party what they are missing. You know, how great a person we are. The false signal does the exact opposite and reinforces our frustration. In fact, it trips the alarm for the other individual that we are adjusting to, and typically that adjustment is received as manipulation. Just as the universe is broadcasting everything at all times to everyone, this signal can be picked up by those in proxy, and create a host of indirect issues with others. The best thing we can do for unsubscribers is accept that our signal is not for everyone and some people just don't want to tune in. We do the exact same thing even if for different reasons. It is not the end of the world if someone chooses to tune us out. Allow it to be their loss and not mutually destructive.

Confidence

The overall purpose of adjusting our frequency is to establish the confidence we need to do the things that we have never done before with our passion. I have come a long way from the place I was in when my personal frequency was transmitting S.O.S. while I tried to look well put together in the face of my peers. One of the things that kept me from writing this book for years was the belief that I was not enough to write at this level. Not good enough, smart enough, experienced enough, educated enough, rich enough, you name it, I was not enough. I lacked the confidence to put pen to paper and fingers to keys. What magnified this challenge was that every time I gathered enough courage to do so, life was more than willing to show up to hold me down.

When I began to change my thoughts, my frequency began to change. I did not start with anything big, just a small blog that I would post a thought of the day on every morning. I used this exercise to give me a central focal point at the very beginning of my day before my doubts and insecurities could wake up. My ascent towards confidence had begun. Each day, regardless of the outcome of the entire day, knowing that I had made one step in the right direction uplifted me. Because I practiced everyday how to best articulate my thoughts, I grew better at it. Though I was sharing those thoughts with the world, my goal was to uplift someone each day, even if that person was only me. The daily thoughts led to more intellectual social media posts and comments, deeper conversations that vibrated at higher levels, and a greater self worth for the value that I bring into the world. What felt surreal about the whole experience to me was that people not only agreed with my perspective, they valued it. All was well, and then out of nowhere, I stopped.

Just as our frequency is in a constant state of flux, our insecurities can come in waves as well. What caused me to stop was that I started to question the value of my own voice. Once again I second guessed if I was enough and as a result, my confidence was low. I am not sure if the person remembers that they did this, but a message from one of the people aligned to my personal broadcast snapped me out of this cycle. They sent me a message asking where my daily thought posts had gone. When I told them why I had not posted them, their response was this: "Never stop sharing your thoughts. Someone, somewhere NEEDS to hear what you have to say!" Insecurities still arise from time to time, but these words have drastically shortened my recovery time.

- **Passion Point:** Not being willing to admit our role in our greatest regrets can cause them to haunt us for a lifetime. Accept accountability to make space for forgiveness.

Adjusting the frequency regarding our passion requires continual effort. It will ebb and flow between peaks of confidence and valleys of insecurity. Becoming efficient with making adjustments as necessary will help us rapidly adapt to changes that have the potential of pushing us backwards. Remember the law of attraction is a twofold process of thoughts and energy. You can choose today to stop making wishes and start working to make those wishes come true. I sincerely believe that people can change if they are willing to learn how to adjust their frequency to receive the signals that they truly desire. Listen to your heart, it tends to know things. Because the truth of the matter is that someone, somewhere does need to hear our thoughts. Even if that someone is us.

NOW HIRING
(Solidify Your Stance and Move Forward)

CHAPTER 9

Create a True North

I n the 1953 Disney classic *Peter Pan*, with the help of pixie dust from Tinkerbell, Peter and the Lost Boys were able to fly. As a child, I always thought that the pixie dust was the magical component that made the group capable of flight. However, it was not until I was much older that I understood that the actual magic resided in each individuals' ability to believe that they themself could fly. The boys could bathe in pixie dust until they twinkled like Tinkerbell herself, but until they believed they could fly, they were grounded. Though we do not have access to pixie dust in today's world, we have still managed to find a way to soar with the birds in the sky.

When you hear the name the Wright brothers, you probably think about the invention of the airplane. Many people think that the Wright brothers invented airplanes, but the fact is there were hundreds of heavier-than-air prototype vehicles long before Orville and Wilbur began their flight endeavors. Lifting these vehicles into the air was actually not impossible for many of their predecessors. The issue was simply staying in the air itself. If the Wright brothers invented anything, it was the mechanism designed to control yaw, roll, and pitch. The brothers believed so deeply that it was possible to control flight, that they risked their own safety to achieve it. During a test flight in 1908, Orville Wright crashed the Wright Model A at Fort Myer, Virginia, killing his passenger Lt. Thomas E. Selfridge. Orville also suffered severe injuries that landed him in the hospital for well over a month. Most people at this point would probably consider giving up, but Orville still believed. In fact, this was actually Orville's fifth major crash and he would experience 3 more crashes as he and his brother pursued their passion for perfecting flight. See, belief has the ability to convict us so strongly that it inspires us to continue our efforts even if we experience failure along the way. It creates certainty about the achievability of our dreams and requires us to find a way to bring them into reality. This is why belief is the first passion mentality that we are going to hire. Let's welcome belief to the team!

Creating Belief

Creating belief around our passion is a continuous cycle of believing in our own greatness, doubting that greatness, and relying on endurance until the full potential of our greatness is achieved. When we believe in something strongly enough, we establish a personal truth around it. Once applied to our passion, personal truth establishes that there is no world that we live in in which our passion does not exist. Think about the power of that statement for a moment. The mere fact that we are present right now means that our passion, whether known or unknown to us, exists. However, to embrace this belief we must first understand how the cycle of belief operates. The best way to illustrate this cycle is by the stages of the day: sunrise to sunset, dusk until midnight, and midnight until dawn.

Cycle of Belief

Belief

Belief, the first part of the cycle of belief, occurs between sunrise and sunset. The moment we adopt a new personal truth, the sky is illuminated with the brightness of the sun. The possibilities appear to be endless as enthusiasm is abundant during this stage. While in the light, we are energized to further bring our passions into the world, and our ideas, actions, and even allies seem to flow effortlessly into this phase. Surprisingly enough, it was the relationship between my eldest son and me that taught me just how important belief is for anything that you want to achieve in life. Especially when it comes to your passion.

Fatherhood has by far been the most difficult role I have ever had the honor to hold. No matter how prepared you think you are the day your child is born, you will never fully comprehend the struggles of guiding that child into adulthood. Though I knew I would make many errors raising my son, the one belief that often kept me from giving up during times of adversity was that I knew I was capable of providing him with a good compass. This took an abundance of pressure off of me as his father. As I became less concerned about failing him, I began to hyper-focus on ensuring that he would have a solid understanding of how to use the tools I had provided him throughout the years. What this meant was, if ever he found himself in a situation that was foreign to him, regardless of the potential outcome, I trusted in the values that I had instilled to guide him true. Whether he actually chose to go in that direction is a completely different story.

Belief is the compass that helps us establish a point of reference for our passion's true North. It allows us to see where we are heading and provides insight as to when we are veering off course. If your dream is to be an elite athlete, belief will guide you to train and condition your body to meet the demands of that level. If you take too many days off or eat outside of your nutrition plan too often, belief can nudge you back on track. In essence, belief keeps us focused on our passion, and where our focus goes, our energy flows. Unfortunately, no matter how great we feel in the belief stage, at some point for one reason or another, the sun sets and we begin to doubt our truths.

- **Passion Point:** When it comes to your passion, what is your truth? What do you believe?

Doubt

Doubt, the second part of the cycle of belief occurs between dusk and midnight. This is where we begin to question if our truth is valid or based upon wishful thinking. During this stage, we spend more energy second-guessing our passion than we do building upon it. As the night grows darker, it can feel as if belief will never rise again. Underlying insecurities about our sense of worthiness can also play a devastating role during this stage. As with all stages in the cycle of belief, there is no set time period assigned to doubt. However, there is a pivotal decision that must be made in order to move to the next stage.

The inevitable question that we all must ask in the doubt stage is whether or not we will continue to believe. Truthfully, belief is the only choice we can make, but what we believe will require commitment. It is from this choice that the rest of the cycle of belief flows. Just to be clear, doubt is a normal part of any extended process. There have been numerous times in the gym when I felt as if I could not complete one more rep. Even as a parent, I have had recurring doubts about my inadequacies as a father. I assure you, we are not alone in our journey through this cycle, and everything we experience, both good and bad throughout this process, is designed to condition us for the third and final stage of the cycle of belief.

Endurance

Endurance, the period between midnight and dawn, is when we begin to pull out of the darkness of the cycle of belief and head once again towards the light. No matter which belief we choose to nurture in the doubt stage, endurance will always play the role of either building or reestablishing the foundation upon which that belief will be placed. If we choose to abandon our former beliefs, we will seek out other existing truths within our identity to support the under-developed beliefs. If we choose to reestablish our original beliefs, we may have to reassess the truths upon which the beliefs were previously attached to determine how we can better insulate them from the effects of doubt and disbelief. As simple as these 2 paths may sound, we sometimes can get stuck in an endurance loop that holds us hostage to this stage for longer than necessary.

Imagine that you woke up early one weekend to catch the sunrise at 6:10 am. At 6:09 am, just before the sun begins to crest the horizon, it changes course and begins to set once again. Rather than experiencing the brightness of a new day, you gradually return to the night. This is exactly what an endurance loop would look like. It is easy to get stuck in the endurance stage and become overwhelmed by feeling as if you are destined to endlessly endure for a sunrise that will never come. The cruel truth is that often, many of us back down right before we break through.

One of the great things about being laid off early in life is that I learned in my teens rather than in my fifties that my job was not guaranteed. By the time I was laid off in 2009 during the housing crisis, I felt no sense of panic when people would ask me what I was going to do. My answer was always the same. I was too young and too broke to retire, so I would have to find another job. I have been without a job before, so I knew that it was not impossible to find another one. Just as with the law of attraction, breaking through the endurance stage of the cycle of belief will require work. We must learn how to draw on the strength found in knowing that we have doubted before, and have made it to a place where our beliefs have risen like a phoenix from the ashes to thrive again. This is the key to breaking through the endurance stage back into the light of belief. It will cause the cycle of belief to come full circle back to new personal truths that will be relied upon in the new cycle.

To understand the cycle of belief is to understand that whenever we are ready, we are capable of being unstoppable. The exciting link to this is that since our passions dwell with and within us, they too are an equally unstoppable force. As we learn how to instinctively identify each stage, it will become more and more a part of our identity. I am certain that in doing so, one day you will realize that you spend less time in the stages of doubt and endurance and more time in the power of your belief.

The Silent Audience

There is another lesson about belief that often goes unmentioned. Brace yourself for a perspective-altering revelation. People are waiting on you to believe in yourself. I know what you are thinking. Your lack of belief is not holding up the show for anyone else's life, but I promise that there are many cases where it is. In order for others to believe in us and our passions, we first have to believe in ourselves. We do not live our lives in isolation. What we bring into the world matters and creates ripples that interact with others. Unfortunately, nowadays, social media has conditioned us to place a higher value on the number of "likes" and "follows" we can acquire. This behavior has impeded our ability to comprehend the importance of how we connect to others. I refer to these connections as our silent audience. These are the people that typically sit back, admire our actions in silence, and draw strength from our courage in order to act on their own beliefs. Unfortunately, not everyone in this audience is rooting for us to win.

If you recall from chapter 7, our passion has both an external and intrinsic value. Though we do not get to choose the value that others place on our passion, we are able to impact their judgment. When we create belief in ourselves regarding our passion, the byproduct of that belief is action. As the actions we take are experienced by others, it can cause their doubts about us and themselves to subside.

When I told my boss that I was an inspirational speaker he told me that he didn't really see me as an inspirational person. Rather than wasting energy on adjusting my frequency to convince him of all the reasons that I am inspirational, I simply acknowledged that I must not be here to inspire him. Later that year when I returned from a speaking engagement, my boss snidely asked me how it went. I responded with one word. "Phenomenal!" With a surprised look on his face, he asked me why I thought it went so well. After explaining the success of the event the next question my boss asked with concern in his voice. "Do you think that you will ever not have enough vacation time to cover going on these speaking engagements?" Wait!? How did we go from me not being an inspirational person, to being concerned if I would run out of vacation time for speaking engagements? What changed? My boss' external value of my ability to inspire initially was set relatively low. I did not know it at the time, but he too was a silent audience member that was waiting for me to fail. However, once he saw the outcome of my actions, he was forced to question his own disbelief.

We can spend a lifetime attempting to prove to others who we are, and never convince them, or we can spend a lifetime being who we are and let those results speak for themselves. I have produced over a hundred YouTube videos with inspirational content. I cannot tell you how many likes I have received over the years, but I can tell you that I have had an abundance of conversations with people who have expressed to me how my videos have helped them or someone close to them. This is the silent audience ripple effect that I am referring to. As a result of my belief that I have an inspirational message, which really was just a public message to myself, that message is now in the hands of strangers operating as a catalyst in their lives. Acting on faith can become contagious as we take the leaps required to pursue our passions. It can inspire others to not only pursue their passions, but can also persuade them to support and value ours.

Toxic Truth

Conditional Truth

The personal truths that belief creates can be powerful allies to our passions, but even they can be fallible at times. Due to the intertwined nature of our truths, we can tend to be overly protective of them at the individual level. Toxic truth is an event that occurs when we hold on to 1 truth because we fear that letting it go will invalidate other ones. Sometimes toxic truth is an actual truth that we have embraced as absolute when in reality it is conditional. Let's take the phrase, "What goes up, must come down." Here on Earth, that phrase used to be an absolute truth. There was a time when we did not possess the technology to debunk this truth, but today it has become subjective to the circumstances in which it is applied. Yes, if we throw a ball into the air, gravity will pull it back to the ground enabling us to catch it. However, imagine if we threw that same ball into outer space. What sense would it make to stand around waiting for it to come back down to catch? At least with this type of toxic truth, you have a chance of the truth applying on occasion. Unfortunately, there is an even more destructive form of toxic truth in which the accepted truth does not apply 100% of the time.

False Narrative Truth

It can be especially crippling when toxic truth is built upon a false narrative that we recognize as false but continue to agree to acknowledge as if it were true. This form of toxic truth typically manifests as self-abuse or in the acceptance of our identity gleaned from personal attacks made by others. How often do we relentlessly beat ourselves up for making mistakes? We say that we are stupid, dumb, and repeat even more damaging mantras that erode our confidence in our intelligence. We know that these things are only being accepted as truth because of our mistakes, but we hold to them anyway. How about allowing ourselves to be taken back to a time when we made a mistake because someone is bashing us about it in the present? Is that really the person you are today? If we hold on to these false narratives for too long, our other healthy truths begin to conform to what we are choosing to accept.

Timeout: Toxic Truth

*Grab your **Passion Journal**. Think about the truths that guide your identity. If you are a strong-willed person, you may believe that you* *cannot interact with hurt emotions, because strong people can't be hurt. If you are an empath and emotionally sensitive, you may not believe that strength is accessible to your identity. Where are you using these types of one-size-fits-all toxic truths in your life? Have some of these truths expired or did they never really exist in the first place?*

Divide a piece of paper in half. On one side, take about 5 minutes to list what you feel are the most positive attributes about your identity. On the other side, take another 5 minutes to list what you feel are the most negative attributes about your identity. Once you have completed both sides, see if you can find any conflicting attributes. For example, if you were loving on your positive side, but indifferent on your negative side, those 2 attributes would conflict. Examine your conflicts and challenge yourself to decide if the attributes are true, conditionally true, or based upon a false/expired narrative. If you identify any conditional truths, work to become clearer on which conditions correlate to that truth and which do not. If you find false/expired narrative truths, work to debunk them and rid your identity from the impact of their lies. I recommend going through this exercise at least once a year, but every 6 months is ideal.

Toxic truth is nothing more than an avoidance coping mechanism designed to circumvent the emotional state of disappointment. Though we did not cover the emotion of disappointment in *chapter 6: Feel, Think, Passion*, simplified it is when we are surprised with unpleasant circumstances or information. Since we do not like to be disappointed, we allow ourselves to believe we are failures. This softens the blow of disappointment when we fail because that is what we expected all along. There is, however, a healthier way to process disappointment without using toxic truth.

I once had a person in an argument bring up one of the lowest moments of my life in an attempt to persuade me to concede my position. The problem was that at the time we were having the argument, my lowest point had occurred over 8 years prior. Though the memory was embarrassing, I responded with this: "If your intent is to use something that I did 8 years ago to manipulate me today, it will never work. I have grown from that experience, and the person you are talking to today is not the same person from 8 years ago." Forgiveness is the healthy alternative to toxic truth. However, forgiveness from others is contingent upon what the other party has received from us and is willing to let go. That space of forgiveness is out of our control, and regardless, we all know our worst critic intimately. Until we learn that forgiveness originates within us, and allow it to be nurtured, we cannot effectively rid ourselves of the waste that toxic truth creates. By accepting our own forgiveness, we are acknowledging our flaws, mistakes, and most importantly, our humanity. In doing so we can accept that decommissioning any truth that no longer serves our identity does not invalidate all the other truths that were once connected to it.

Belief is the cornerstone of our passion's foundation. It unlocks our passion by disabling our perceived limitations. As we improve upon our mastery of belief, we not only increase the chances of fulfilling our passion, but we also operate as a beacon of hope for those who are just embarking on their journey. As I stated in the opening prescription, we are practicing today for who we want to be tomorrow. If that is truly the person we desire to be, then we must believe our way to that identity.

CHAPTER 10

A Journey of 1,000 Steps

Growing up, anytime my family took a vacation it always meant one thing. Road trip. This was not like the road trips of today where children have electronics to keep them entertained throughout the duration of the trip. When my family piled into the car for a road trip, our primary sources of entertainment were each other, the windows, or sleep. Most of the time we would start on the road just before daylight, so for the first hour or so, my sister and I would sleep in the backseat. A few conversations about what we would do once we arrived at our destination, a couple of games of eye spy, and our other 2 forms of entertainment had also been exhausted. At this point boredom quickly set in, and it felt as if the drive began to take days rather than hours. I am sure that you could guess what impatient question came next. Are we there yet?

Like the road trips during my childhood, our passion is a journey of steps that must be traveled in order to reach our destination. When we give each moment in the journey a purpose, our focus on the time and miles melt away. In this space, lessons are learned and skills are acquired and developed. However, when we ignore the journey and only focus on the destination, we allow impatience to set in. This can cause our journey to feel sluggish and become frustrating. If we can learn how to value the journey just as much as we value the destination, each step towards our passion can empower the next.

That is why the next passion mentality we are going to hire is enjoyment. Welcome aboard.

The Passion Game

Think about how likely we would be to pursue our passion if it made us miserable every step of the way. Probably not very likely, right? The odds against us are doubled when we feel like we consistently take steps that lead us in the wrong direction. Enjoyment is the passion mentality that keeps us engaged. It can help transform the work that we *have* to do into the work we *want* to do. There are multiple ways to extract enjoyment out of the journey towards our passion, but my favorite method is by making a game out of the process.

While learning how to multiply in elementary school, they introduced a math-based game called Number Munchers. Many of us did not particularly like sitting in class going over multiplication problems, but when the computer came on in the back of the room, there was always a line to play the game. In the game, while being chased by monsters that were trying to eat you, your character the Number Muncher would rush to eat all the numbers that were multiples of a specific number. The better you were at the game, the longer you played. What none of us realized was that at the same time as we were getting better at the game, we were simultaneously getting better at multiplication. This same game mentality can be applied to the journey towards our passion.

Tiny Victories

In order to turn our passion into a game, we must first realize that achieving our passion is not made up of a singular victory, but rather an accumulation of multiple tiny victories. By embracing this concept, the step we make today is now just as meaningful as the last step we take to arrive at our destination. Since we are playing multiple mini-games that are interconnected by days, let's set a daily rule for our passion game. The universal rule of the game is this: no matter what happens on any given day, we are obligated to find a way to win. Winning is not determined by whether or not we get the steps right, that part is irrelevant. As long as we can take a lesson with us from today into tomorrow we will always win.

By injecting enjoyment along the way, the daily game mentality helps us fall in love with the process of striving for our passion and not just its destination. It ensures that we arrive at our passion with more than just a shell of what we believe our passion is supposed to look like on the outside. In fact, if all we are is a shell, we will never arrive at our passion. It is just like, no matter how long a hen incubates an empty shell, a baby chick will never hatch. Our journey to bring our passion into existence is what provides the internal content necessary to bring that passion to life.

Create a Bond to the Present

The greatest benefit that enjoyment brings to our passion is that it creates a bond to the present. The increase in our connection to what we can affect in real-time not only provides a greater level of satisfaction but also unlocks other indirect benefits that serve our passion immensely. These indirect benefits are gratitude, memory highlights, and clarity. As we deepen our bond to the present it is these indirect benefits that act as the roots that hold our feet sure to the path towards our passion.

Gratitude

Through good times and bad, there is no tool more powerful than gratitude. By connecting to the present, we learn to appreciate being a part of the process of watching our passion unfold right before our eyes. Being a part of the process also means that we have some control of where it goes. I had the opportunity to watch this in-the-moment gratitude recently as my niece competed in a Premier

Girls Fastpitch National Tournament. You can imagine, with the best teams from across the nation, the competition was fierce. However, as I sat and observed my niece game after game, I realized that gratitude is not always the warm and fuzzy experience we hope for it to be.

It never mattered if my niece's team was up or down, she showed up on every play, just grateful to be a part of the experience, give it her all, and continue to build upon her dreams. This is what a person who carries a gratitude mindset does. Regardless of the present circumstances, whenever there is an opportunity to do so, they show up. After all, if we allow the difficult parts of our life to discourage us and we quit every time the going gets rough, can we truly be grateful for the opportunities we have to show up? During the tournament, my niece made errors and even struck out a couple of times, because that is also a part of the process. We all know personally how frustrating this part can be, but if we can remain present and grateful even in these moments then we will activate our ability to change our perspective. This is when, rather than seeing challenges as obstacles designed to impede our journey towards our passion, we embrace them as opportunities to grow, overcome, and strengthen our abilities for the next step.

Memory Highlights

Another benefit that creating a bond to the present presents is that it establishes memory highlights. Think about how many experiences you have had in your lifetime. Now how many of those memories stand out? Why? The answer for the majority of the highlights is that you were present in the experience. It is hard for many people to remember events that they were not present for either physically or mentally. As a student, I struggled with remembering dates of events in history, because other than reading about them in books, I was not present for them. Come to think about it, I actually was not very present in history class either. Now if you ask me today what time my first son was born 19 years ago, I have no doubt in my ability to answer that question. The difference between U.S. history and the birth of my son is that I was present both physically and mentally at the moment of his birth.

Multitasking

It is impossible to be present and distracted at the same time. No matter how great of a multitasker we think we are, we can only truly focus on one thing at a time. I like to play instrumentals when I write. The music helps me by blocking out the distracting noises in my environment and keeps my mind centered on the development of my ideas. As often as I have used this strategy to write, I cannot associate a single song to any specific writing that I have completed. In fact, when I reflect on my memories of writing, I often remember silence even though I know it is likely that music was playing. This is because there is a difference between hearing music and listening to it.

Hearing music is an automated task, one the mind is capable of blocking out. Though music is present, it is not fully integrated as a part of our experience. Listening on the other hand is an intentional task, one on which the mind is designed to focus upon. Because I am present with writing, but only hearing the music at the moment, my mind is only capable of accessing relevant memories and not the automated tasks surrounding them.

Interruption

The only way an automated task can become a highlight is if it abruptly shifts into an intentional one. Many parents can attest to sitting in a park hearing multiple kids playing while they are having conversations with other parents. Hearing the kids play is background noise until we hear crying cut through the ordinary ambiance. The sound of crying pulls us immediately into intentionality. Often, we will completely forget what we were even talking about, and the newly identified situation typically becomes the focal point of the memory.

As we strive to reach our passion, our memory highlights will act as checkpoints along the way. These checkpoints enable us to quickly access the information that we need to create applicable solutions, make healthy choices, and keep a steady trajectory towards our passion. When we lack these memory highlights, the further away we are from the initial event the more difficult it can be to tap into the knowledge we have stored in our memory. By practicing bonding to the present, we help to ensure that our memory highlights are readily available and are associated with the most meaningful moments in our lives.

Clarity

On a clear night, when you look up in the sky you may see what appears to be a reddish-orange star. If you were to look at that star through a telescope, you would find that what your eyes are actually seeing is the planet Mars. The telescope's ability to remove the visual distance between Earth and Mars produces clarity of the actual object. Our bond with the present also creates clarity in a similar manner.

For many of us, our passion is so many steps away that we can barely even see it. Bonding with the present helps us to remove the distance between us and our experiences, and as a result, diminishes the visual distance between us and our passion. The closer we are to our experiences, the more purposeful those experiences can become. For instance, a terrible event can happen halfway around the world from where you live. You may have a generic connection or be indifferent to that event, but you choose not to be involved. However, if that same event happened to your next-door neighbor, your connection would be amplified because it was closer to your home. With this event, you might feel a sense of urgency to provide assistance. When we are closer with our experiences we not only understand them more fluently, but we are also more prone to personally invest in them. Establishing clarity will help to better equip us by determining what types of attributes, skills, and even relationships will align with our passion. With this information, we can invest in our passion today in a more meaningful manner.

Timeout: Does it look like it fits?

*Grab your **Passion Journal**. The benefit of being able to see your passion sooner rather than later is that you can hold up ideas that you have about it ahead of time. Ask yourself if your present activities fit what you imagine your passion to be. On a piece of paper draw 4 different sized triangles. In the first and third triangles write the word "Passion." In the second and fourth triangles write the word "Activities." Now match the first triangle with the second, and the third with the fourth. In your groups which triangle is larger, your passion or your activities? Does your passion fit into your activities? What needs to grow or shrink? Does a triangle need to be eliminated altogether? If you got lucky, on at least one of your activity triangles your passion triangle was able to fit with room for your passion to grow.*

Now let's repeat this exercise, but this time use something that you are passionate about in the first triangle, and the activities you are doing to meet the needs of that passion in the second triangle. Do those activities fit or does it look like you are rowing a boat in the middle of a desert? If your passion fits and has room for expansion, you are in a great position! If it feels like your passion is greater than your activities, explore where you see your passion going and either how you can incorporate more relevant activities, or retire the passion altogether.

Shortcuts

In any journey, there is a point when an opportunity to take a shortcut may arise. Shortcuts can help to close the physical distance between us and our passion. Often when people hear the word shortcut they automatically associate it with easier. However, shortcuts are not always easier. In fact, they are often more difficult to navigate and less forgiving of mistakes. If all shortcuts were easy, everyone would use them, and that would just become the standard path that we all would take. So how do we determine if a shortcut is right for our passion journey?

Unfortunately, most shortcuts are forks in the road where we can either go left or right. Since we cannot travel both paths simultaneously, a decision has to be made. The very first step to determining if a shortcut is right for us is to take inventory that we have all the necessary supplies to effectively succeed. Going back to family road trips. If we can take a path that cuts 2 hours off of our trip, but we don't have enough fuel to make it to the next gas station on that path, that is not a shortcut for us. The problem is that many of us are impulsive when it comes to taking shortcuts. We allow ourselves to be blinded by all of the benefits the shortcut has to offer, but do not analyze the challenges that will be introduced by it. As a result, we end up somewhere in the middle of the shortcut stranded, and our journey takes even longer than it would have if we just stayed on the original path.

The second thing to consider with every shortcut is the risk that you are signing up for. Remember, shortcuts can be less forgiving than the beaten path. Heavily consider the potential consequences that come with unsuccessfully navigating the shortcut. If the price is too great for our risk tolerance, we might be better served passing up on the opportunity. This will save us from the anxiety that comes with being too far outside of our comfort zone. Extenuating stress can create unnecessary fatigue on our journey, wearing down the energy that we need to arrive at our passion. Yes, without risk there can be no reward, but you are not obligated to go all-in.

Lastly, as with any opportunity, avoid the glaringly too-good-to-be-true shortcuts. Those are the ones that typically lead us all the way back to the beginning of our journey. We can typically trust our conscience when it feels like something is not right or is out of place. Furthermore, we shouldn't allow pressure from others or even ourselves to push us to take a path that we really don't want to go down. It is ok to miss out on some shortcuts. Maybe there is just more that we need on the standard path or we just have not arrived at the short-cut that is right for us.

Whether our path uses shortcuts or not, there is no substitute for the distance we will have to cover. Remember that in a journey of steps, enjoyment is the key to the process. We should check in daily to determine how we can best appreciate the steps that we will take today. As we continue to enjoy the process of pursuing our passion, our growth will begin to feel automated. From day to day we will forget the necessary work that we put in to arrive at our passion. However, when we look back we will clearly be able to see when our steps became progress, our progress became leaps, and those leaps landed us at our passion. We might as well enjoy the ride while it lasts.

CHAPTER 11

Challenge Impossibilities

When we think of overcoming incredible odds we probably think about Hollywood blockbusters like Marvel's *The Avengers*, *300*, or maybe even the Tom Hanks' classic *Forrest Gump*. These types of movies take the audience on an emotional rollercoaster in which, just when we feel that giving up is the only option, the character finds a way to push through adversity, save the day, or achieve their dreams. Though our lives may not be as well-written as some of these movie scripts, our journey of passion is bound to run into roadblocks along the way that we must solve in order to forge ahead.

When NBA small forward Paul George broke his leg in August 2014, I remember thinking that it was the end of his NBA career. At the time George was attempting to earn a spot on the 2016 Olympic team and had just come off the best year of his professional career. During the 2013 - 2014 regular season, pre-injury George averaged 21.7 points per game, 36.4% three-point shooting, and a 20.16 player efficiency rating. I know they say when you break a bone, it can become even stronger than prior to the break, but when George returned to the league for the 2015 - 2016 regular season he was nothing short of a beast. George's stats that season improved in almost every category. He averaged 23.1 points per game, 37.1% three-point shooting, and increased his player efficiency rating to 26.19. How was George able to return to the game more powerful than before his injury? George embraced what I refer to as an over-comer spirit. In spite of the odds that were stacked against him, he decided that he was not going to allow the injury to be the end of his story. The overcomer spirit is the next passion mentality that we need to hire to ensure the challenges that await us do not keep us from reaching our passion.

The 5 Keys to Overcoming the Impossible

As we delve deeper into our passions, obstacles are bound to appear. Sometimes the obstacle can be a small hill, and other times it can feel as if it is higher than Mt. Everest. Either way, we are going to run into some snags along the way. To possess an overcomer spirit means that we are committed to not allowing roadblocks to block our path forever. Obstacles in our passion journey are nothing more than challenges we have yet to solve. Once we come up with a solution for them, we are able to move forward and they look smaller as they disappear in our rearview mirror. Though the solutions that we come up with are not one size fits all, there are 5 keys that I have learned to carry in order to help overcome impossible odds.

Don't Stop

The first key to embrace is only stop if you absolutely have to. Newton's first law of motion regarding objects that are at rest high-lights why this is important. If you have ever had to push a stalled vehicle, you know that the hardest part is getting it going. Once the car begins to roll, it takes considerably less effort to keep it rolling in a straight line. Newton's law states that an object in motion remains in motion at a constant speed until it is acted upon by an unbalanced force. It is hard to move the car initially because it is at rest, and until we overpower that force, it will remain at rest.

Like the stalled vehicle, our challenges sit at rest waiting for us to overwhelm them into motion. Fortunately for us, before we arrive at a challenge, we ourselves are in motion. If we can avoid stopping unnecessarily, we will go into adversity with momentum. Though the momentum might not be enough to carry us all the way through the challenge, it can give us a pretty good head start. However, as I said before this is not a one size fits all approach. If you are running full speed at a brick wall, it is best that you stop before you hit it to determine the best method to move past it. If the obstacle is a building, rather than coming in like a wrecking ball, maybe we just need to knock or try the doorknob first. Approach challenges accordingly.

Obstacles are Not Exclusive

The second key to carry with us is to embrace that we are not the first person to experience resistance while forging a path towards our passion. In fact, challenges arise for all of us, it is a process known as life. It is harder to overcome challenges when we approach them with a victim mentality. This is because a victim is at the mercy of the external power of other things. Don't spend a lot of time sulking as if the world has decided to single us out in order to make things harder for us and us alone. We all have mountains that we have to climb, and the fact that we are standing at the base of one, simply means that it is our turn to take out our climbing gear and get to work.

You Can't Ignore a Challenge Away

The third key to carry is the fact that a challenge will not go away simply because it is being ignored. Think about how incredible the odds for survival are when cancer is discovered early. Our odds to overcome challenges also greatly improves the faster we can recognize the challenge exists. Similar to how our body presents symptoms when something is wrong, challenges typically do the same to announce their presence. Sometimes the symptoms start off as a minor inconvenience, in the same way, a cold can start with a small sniffle. Unlike a cold that will inevitably run its course, challenges rarely sort themselves out. Ignoring adversity can cause obstacles to gain strength and solidify. If anything, we should be celebrating that we reached the level in our journey where we are now experiencing challenges.

Celebrate Challenges

The fourth key to carry is to remember to celebrate your challenges. This may seem counterintuitive, but hear me out. In order for us to arrive at a challenge on the road to our passion, we have to arrive at a place beyond our current abilities. You should recall how we made our passion into a game in the last chapter? This is the part of the game where we unlock new tools and abilities. As we level up we become stronger, faster, smarter, and more deeply convinced that we can achieve anything we put our efforts into.

Don't Allow Failure to be the Last Time

The fifth and final key is to make stopping and staying at failure 100% unacceptable. Failure only becomes a permanent experience when we choose to allow it to be. Rather than adopting the thought process that things are impossible to fix, what if they were impossible to break. We stop at failure when we start to believe that maybe we don't belong with success, maybe we don't deserve to be there, or we are somehow unworthy of its achievement. Of course, challenges are difficult, they wouldn't be challenging if they weren't. However, just because something is difficult the first hundred or so attempts does not mean we should give up. To avoid indefinite failure we should only stop when we must and go when we can. I can promise that there will be times when we will roll back down the mountain and find ourselves right back at its base and that is ok. What is most important is that we don't stay there waiting to somehow teleport past the mountain altogether. Dust yourself off, pick up your tools, and start moving. I'd rather die trying to succeed than live a life where failure has supreme rule over my efforts.

With these 5 keys, there is no challenge that we cannot unlock a solution for. Each time we use a key we are intentionally choosing to not allow an obstacle to be the end of our story, but simply a transitive segment of it. Through consistent effort, eventually, we will develop the means to overwhelm the obstacle with force or adapt the intelligence necessary to outsmart the obstacle altogether. Either way, impossible challenges are only impossible until we create the possibilities to overcome them. Though this is the foundation of how to obtain an overcomer spirit, there are some other actions that we must fully engage with in order to become overcomers.

Leave Nothing in the Tank

In the Bellator 265 heavyweight main event, Cheick Kongo was knocked down a couple of times by punches landed by Sergei Kharitonov. Kongo, at the age of 46, was the oldest fighter in Bellator at the time. In a surprising turn of events in the second round of the fight, Kongo was able to take Kharitonov to the ground, where after landing some significant damage, he was able to secure a submission victory with about 1 second left in the round. What happened next was a lesson that we all could learn from. Rather than getting up to celebrate, Kongo rolled over on his back lying on the ring floor for the next 3 minutes in sheer exhaustion. With about 46 seconds left in the second round, Kongo made a critical decision to leave nothing in the tank. At that moment he decided, win or lose, he was committing all of his energy to finish the fight.

When we come across these types of all-or-nothing moments during impossible challenges, we must be willing to squeeze out every drop of energy to reach the climax of the event. If we give up with reserves left in the tank we condition ourselves to create behaviors that in turn cause us to give up when things are difficult rather than temporarily impossible. This is the equivalent of pulling over your car in the middle of nowhere and deciding to walk because you have a ¼ tank of gas that will not take you successfully to the next gas station. Common sense would dictate that we drive as close as we can in the car and then walk the rest of the way to the gas station, but it is surprising how many of us take the alternate approach when pursuing our passions.

Sometimes you can give your all and even that is not enough, but failure under these circumstances still comes as a benefit to the overcomer spirit. Each time we fully deplete our energy, we make a little more space to fill up the next time around. It is like sprinting on a treadmill. If each time you sprint you consistently do so until you no longer can, each subsequent time you sprint you will go farther and farther. Track athletes do not start off sprinting 400 meters, they work their way up to it. Leaving nothing in the tank is a decision of whether we want to increase the capacity of our resilience or diminish it. Each time we choose to put it all on the line, we are acknowledging that though what we have today may not be enough to reach our passion, we are always capable of being more than enough eventually.

Their Limitations, Not Yours

After suffering a disabling injury in the military, Veteran Arthur Boorman was told by doctors that it would be impossible for him to walk unassisted ever again. For 15 years of his life, Arthur accepted this limitation as one in which he would never be able to overcome. I think many of us in his circumstances would assume that the doctors knew what they were talking about in regards to his limitations. However, Arthur decided that he wanted more for his quality of life. Over the next 10 months, Arthur underwent an amazing transformation and not only lost 140 pounds, but regained his ability to walk and run. Fifteen years is a long time to live under limitations set by someone else. It was not until Arthur decided that he would be the author of his limitations that he was able to shed his hopelessness and grab ahold of hope.

Timeout: Keep Striving for Someday

*Grab your **Passion Journal**. Besides his ability to regain mobility, there was one other thing that stood out to me about Arthur's story. He said, "Just because I can't do it today, doesn't mean that I can't do it someday." Take some time to think about a current impossible challenge in your life. List some of the symptoms that let you know it is there. Try to identify the actual issue. You may have tried to overcome this challenge multiple times to no avail, but make a commitment to take a crack at it every opportunity you get the chance to. Though people may tell you that you are wasting your time, keep in mind that your limitations are yours to set and strongly based upon your beliefs. If today is not the day you achieve victory, continue to strive for someday. Review why you may have failed and determine if you were addressing the symptoms or the actual issue. Try to take the salvable pieces and create a new plan to address the issue. Most importantly, don't be discouraged to try again. Repeat this exercise each time that you encounter a challenge that you fail to overcome. You will find that sometimes there are only little tweaks that need to be made, and other times you need a whole new approach. Remember that impossible is only impossible until it isn't.*

Arthur's story really started me thinking about the limitations that we experience in our lives and the importance of identifying where they come from. Specifically, is this a limit that we create based upon the intimate knowledge and insight that we have about our life? Or is this a general limitation applied to the masses that we have decided to apply, even though it is inapplicable to us? From time to time I struggle with general limitations regarding the fact that I do not currently possess a college degree. There is so much information about the success rate of those who have a degree over their peers who only have a high school diploma that one could easily drown in the statistics. The one statistic that stood out to me early in my career was the difference in earning potential between the two categories. In many cases, the income variance was significantly tangible. However, those limitations that I incorporated from others did not take into account my personal situation. I have a strong work ethic, am resourceful, great at building business relationships, and I'm huge on learning new things outside of a classroom environment. These attributes changed my earning limitations and as I embraced them, I found my worth to be far above the statistical average.

Another way to look at the limitations of others can be found in the story of the city of Troy and the Trojan horse. The city of Troy was protected by massive walls which were a major obstacle to King Agamemnon's army during their attack. However, the Trojans did not feel safe behind their walls because of King Agamemnon's failed efforts to breach them. The origin of Trojan safety came based upon their own perceived inability to overcome the defenses that they had established. Unfortunately, King Agamemnon's abilities superseded the Trojan's own limitations when he was able to devise a plan that later allowed him to overcome the obstacle presented by the walls. As I mentioned earlier in this chapter, you can either overpower or outsmart an obstacle. Where brute force failed, cunning prevailed. In a facade, King Agamemnon's army made it appear as if they abandoned the siege of Troy and left behind a wooden horse as a gift to receive safe passage on their voyage back across the Aegean Sea. Inside the horse was a small group of men that were tasked with opening the front gate for the greater force waiting beyond the walls. The Trojans' limitations never allowed them to come up with a plan where a small group would be able to open the gate from the inside and as a result, the impossible walls became an open front door for King Agamemnon's army.

Working within our own limits dulls the potency of the impact that the limits others have on our lives. Because we know what we are capable of, even if we are not presently capable of it, we will choose not to sell ourselves short by stopping where someone else would. We dare to embark into their unexplored territories, allowing ourselves to build an identity that is rooted in the surety that comes with understanding our own self-worth and thus producing self-confidence. It is this confidence that ensures that we are only obligated to the limits that we choose to believe, and none of the limits that others have established for themselves. Going forward, every time someone tells you that you cannot do something, simply smile and accept the challenge that your limits are not theirs to set as you smash through their impossible.

Hiring an overcomer spirit is probably the best thing we can do to prepare for the challenges that lay ahead. As we continue to pursue our passion it is our relationship with the overcomer spirit that will inevitably keep our beliefs intact. Though there are never any guarantees in life, by being unwilling to give up in the face of adversity we give ourselves a fighting chance at achieving success. Remember to carry your 5 keys to help overcome impossible challenges and you should be able to unlock the next level of who you need to become to experience all that your passion has to offer.

CHAPTER 12

An Unapologetic Pursuit

In 2018, Lamar High School student Michael Brown, an exceptionally bright and gifted senior, submitted 20 applications to various college universities across the United States. To put this event into perspective, the average student applies to about 8 colleges, typically broken down between 2 colleges the student knows that they can get into, 4 colleges that they want to get into, and 2 colleges that would be nice to get into. Out of the 8 colleges, a student should have 3 - 4 choices as to which school they will attend. Michael's story turned out to be a little different.

The first glaring difference was that Michael applied to twice as many colleges than the average student. That step alone potentially increased his odds at having more choices than his peers. The second and most significant difference in Michael's story was that he was accepted to all 20 colleges with full ride scholarships. As you could imagine a story this rare, and of this magnitude made national news. Most of the coverage on Michael's story was positive, praising him for the results of his hard work and wishing him success for the future. Unfortunately, the Fox 5 DC News team decided to take a different approach in their coverage of Michael's story. Co-anchor Holly Morris and contributor Sarah Fraser chose to mock Michael's accomplishments and actually referred to the fact that he applied to 20 colleges as "obnoxious." How could this negativity be associated with such a feel-good moment?

Unwittingly, Michael stumbled upon a powerful ally that we too can align with our passion. That ally is the power of disruption. It was the disruption from the ordinary that transformed the perspective of Michael from a person who was accepted by 20 colleges into an "obnoxious" overachieving teenager. It will be this same type of disruption that removes our passive-aggressive approach to our passion, and replaces it with an intentionally obsessive one that supercharges the results of our passion. This is exactly why disruption will be the next passion mentality that we hire.

Disrupt the Status Quo

Disruption occurs when we attempt to alter something from its current state. Most of the time when we think about the term disruption, we adopt a negative association with it. For instance, a car accident can cause your entire day to be disrupted as you attempt to take care of the unplanned event. In this light, a disruption is not something that we desire to experience. We are content with the status quo, driving, and want to continue to do so without the headaches that come with an accident. These types of disruptions are the ones that we want to avoid altogether, and rightfully so. However, disruption has the potential to be both positive or negative, and once we understand positive disruption, we can begin to use disruption to our advantage.

Disruption Starts with Us

Often our focus on disruption comes after the disruption has occurred. As a result, disruption typically catches us off guard and ill prepared for what it brings. But what if we could plan for our disruptions to serve us, or better yet our passion? Well we can. The secret to positive disruption is that it originates within us, and as it is with many things that originate in us, it can be harnessed before it is experienced by the world around us. Let's go back to Michael Brown to see how this happens.

Long before he made the decision to apply to 20 colleges, Michael was creating the ripples that would later become the waves to his growth. I am certain that there were times when he could have been outside with friends, scrolling through social media, or playing games online, but he chose to intentionally disrupt those activities from time-to-time by volunteering in his community and honing his academic craft. With this mindset, Michael's disruptions became less about the unforeseen, and more about how he could strategically align his activities with the vision that he had for his future. We too can create a relationship of growth between disruption and our passion simply by identifying the greatest benefit that complacency has to offer, and then comparing it to the greatest benefit we associate with living our passion.

The Complacent Benefit

Long - Term Complacency

The greatest benefit we derive from complacency is a predictable routine. I cannot think of anyone, self included, that has not fallen victim at least once in their life to the intoxicating effects of knowing what is on the other side of each day-to-day activity. The effects are so powerful that sometimes people stay in unhealthy routines, mundane jobs, or within a 5-mile radius of their home simply because they know what to expect. My anger management counselor, Claudia Diaz, referred to this as "familiar shit" syndrome (I am certain that is not the medical term for it). Though the circumstances stink, are filthy, and toxic, we still choose to stay in them and roll around because at the end of the day we feel a sense of perverted pride in ownership of at least something that provides consistency in our life.

As cozy as our complacency can be, when we linger in it for too long it can create both physical and mental damage. If addressed early enough, physical damage can often be rectified quickly. However, once mental damage begins to occur we have a completely different project on our hands. I believe that complacent people do not wake up in the morning with a plan on how they can remain complacent. Many of us get stuck in complacency because we have surrendered to the belief that today is as good as life is going to get for us. Though long before we throw up our white flag, there are some check-point symptoms that tend to appear along the way. Anxiety, depression, and low self-worth are among a few of the symptoms that can arise prior to complacency. These symptoms feed our desire to remain in our comfort zone for the shelter that it provides from their negative effects. The trade off is that in order to remain protected from the negative effects of these symptoms, we are not allowed to move outside the confines of our current square. As a result, prolonged complacency makes us a prisoner to the never-ending experiences of yesterday. What no one tells us is that inevitably these symptoms break right back into our lives, and once inside the concrete walls of the prison, their amplified impact demands that we further retreat into mediocrity.

Short - Term Complacency

Complacency was never intended to be more than a temporary shelter. However, the challenge is that once we get comfortable it can be hard for us to start things moving again. Though the prolonged impact of complacency does not serve our passion well, short-term complacency has the potential to create a healthy space for recovery, reflection, and redefinition. By intentionally moving into a familiar place, the pressures that we are under during growth subside just long enough for us to take a breath, recenter, and pick back up where we left off.

Imagine that you were driving on a freeway to a place that you have never been to before. You don't have GPS, directions, or a map. It is just you and the open road. Without any information, how would you know if you were on the correct freeway, and even if you were, you definitely would not know which exit to take. This is how many of us end up in these long-term complacent engagements. We go into complacency with no idea of what it is that we are looking to receive from it, so we have no way to identify the exit ramps that will lead us to the healthy destination that we seek. If we want to be successful in navigating this experience we have to do what I refer to as setting the alarm.

Setting the alarm is a process that is used to understand that we are attempting to get out of complacency, so that way when we see it, we can exit our comfort zone and move back into our growth-inspired actions. Let's say we think we need a 15-minute break before going back to work. After 15 minutes goes by, we at least know to check in with ourselves to see if that was adequate enough to meet the need. We may find that what we really needed was to take a break for the rest of the day and start fresh tomorrow. Either way, by setting an alarm or some type of notification, even when we decide to continue on the freeway, we at least are aware of what the next checkpoint looks like. The plan does not have to be perfect, but it does have to be in place to ensure that we do not aimlessly wander down the highway while passing all of the exits designed to help us get back on track.

- **Passion Point:** Are you creating a Temporary Shelter or Prison?

Passion Benefit

No matter what our passion is, the greatest benefit we receive from it is fulfillment. There are tons of things that we can do on any given day, but just because we do them does not ensure that they benefit us. How our passion is different is that when we are engaged with it, we are doing what we were designed to do, and that adds value to us. It's like a wrench being used to tighten a bolt versus being tossed as a frisbee. When we are in alignment, our growth is able to soar from level to level in a less encumbered manner. When we are out of alignment with our purpose, our experience with growth can feel sluggish, clunky, or even overwhelming. This book is a great example of how being engaged with my passion for inspirational writing has not only made me more attentive to the everyday lessons that life has to offer, but it has simultaneously increased my self worth as I have learned to apply those lessons to my life.

So now that we know the greatest benefit of both complacency and passion, which benefit do you feel is most important? I hope that your answer was both. If we are going to be serious about hiring our passion, we must know when to disrupt it in order to recharge and avoid burnout. On the other hand, to avoid the complications of long-term complacency, we must know how to effectively disrupt ourselves out of it in a timely manner, so that we can continue to add value to our passion. By creating these positive disruptions we can harness their power and apply them to the larger task of disrupting the world around us.

Changing You Changes the World

About 4 years ago, I experienced a life-changing disruption in regards to my employment. I had submitted a 3-week notice of resignation and it was my last day at the company I had worked at for the past 8 years. All the knowledge that I had acquired to do my job, the stable routine that I had created for myself, and the relationships I had built over the years were all about to change. The scariest part for me was that there was no savings or unemployment safety net in place to catch me. I knew that I was going from a decent income to $0, yet there I was, willing to jump with both feet into uncertainty.

It was during this time in my life that I learned that our passion is not only meant to disrupt and incite change within us, but also the world around us. Though I provided standard operating procedures for my team to follow, my absence created a greater disruption in the office as a whole. Later I found that for many of my peers, watching me leave helped give them the courage to pursue other opportunities for themselves. In addition to the impact on my peers, I now realize that the book *Fire Your Job, Hire Your Passion*, which was also inspired by this event will now allow me to share the lessons I have learned from the experience with the world.

In order for our passion to disrupt the world around us, we must harness enough internal energy to pursue it unapologetically. This means that even when we face fear of judgement and rejection, we make the exposure of our passion to the world non-negotiable. When we take a non-negotiable stance with our passion, we become less timid about putting it on display. Not in the sense of boastfully showing off our passion, but in a manner that enables our passion to disrupt others by way of inspiration.

I have learned that the only way to get better at changing the world is by actually changing it. It is not solely about the words that we speak, but the actions we take to bring those words to life. Unfortunately, even if our passion changes the world for the better, not everyone may be eager to celebrate it. Whether you walk into a pool or do a cannonball into it, it is impossible for your entry to not disturb the surface of the water. No matter how subtle or insignificant it may feel, every time we allow our passion to engage with the world, the world changes. Many people don't like the discomfort that change brings, so don't be surprised if you ruffle a couple of feathers as you begin to make your passion known. During these times, it is important to remember that you do not help people grow when you are only willing to make them comfortable. In fact, there is no faster way to reach compassion fatigue for others than by placing a higher priority on their complacency than you do on your own passion.

Imagine the level of disruption that I had to experience to move away from the foundation that I was never supposed to quit a job before I had another job. This was drilled into me by my parents during my adolescence, and as well intentioned as the advice was, it made it impossible for me to jump into my passion while keeping one foot firmly planted on the ground. It wasn't until I committed to the action of jumping that it even occurred to me that I could fire a job rather than simply quit it. Even when that commitment led to me being alone in another state, it was in this loneliest moment that I became the author of my own fate and began the journey to write my greatest adventure yet. I figure, if we are going to get wet either way, we might as well make a splash, so cannonball it is.

When it comes to our passion, maximum disruption should be the goal. By seeking to introduce as many planned disruptions as often as we can, we ensure that we consistently have access to a healthy space to foster growth. Whether pulling ourselves out of long-term complacency, or intentionally entering short-term complacency, never be afraid to shake things up. Each time we do, the positively energized component of our passion realigns us with the realization that our passion is meant to change the world. It is only right that we pursue that change unapologetically.

CHAPTER 13

A Passion Driven Life

A crucial component of our identity is where we come from. It not only shapes our perspective of the world as to what we have to offer it, but what it has to offer us as well. The neighborhood I grew up in was a tough one. On any given day it could offer love, compassion, violence, or conflict. As challenging as it was to navigate, this complexity taught me many lessons early in life. How to be aware of the things that are going on around me, how to stand up for myself both verbally and physically, even how far in life I could go when I committed to a decision to do so. These lessons continue to help to shape who I am today. There is a saying that most of us are familiar with, "Never forget where you come from." For many people this saying means that we should never be "too good" for where we started. Unfortunately, when we adopt this mindset, our origin can become our anchor. As such, we are tethered to it, and if we do move beyond its boundaries, we drag along with us the heavy burden of survivor's guilt. I recently changed what this saying means to me, and if you'd like, you are welcome to adopt this revised definition as well.

Rather than being a prisoner to my origin, I have decided to use it as a point of reference reflecting how far I have traveled from where I began. This does not mean that I cannot go back to my origin to give back to my community, it just means that I am not obligated to hold onto antiquated perspectives through an awkward sense of duty to my identity. This shift in definition has allowed me to transform my anchor to my neighborhood into an odometer, thus freeing me to transfer my identity anchor to a much more meaningful source, passion. By making this transition to a passion-based identity I discovered authentic evolution and further transformed into who I truly desire to be. After so many years of firing and hiring identities, the time had finally come to hire my greatest identity yet. It was now time for me to hire my passion.

Passion Centric

When we hire our passion we are committing to organically infusing it within our day-to-day lives. I say organically because passion is not something that we have to force. There can be times in which our passion feels unnatural, which typically correlates with seasons of growth, but it should never feel like we are attempting to fit a square peg into a round hole. Whether we are at work, recreation, relaxing, or partaking in any other types of activities, we must embrace the courage necessary to allow our passion to take center stage in our life. Remember that by sharing our passion we will deepen our connection with the world around us, and by doing so add value to the people we encounter along the way.

Symptoms of Passion

As a child, I was extraordinarily curious about how things worked. Whether I was taking apart toys or making makeshift traps for snowball fights, my childhood in many ways was one big experiment. Strangely enough, my greatest subject of curiosity was people. Not so much their opinions, but I was more so inquisitive about their lives in general. I recall many times sitting in the backseat peering out the window as my parents drove down the freeway, thinking to myself about the backstory for each person in the vehicles that we passed enroute to our destination. Where were they going? What was their life like? My mind was a sea of questions about who they were.

BILLY F. WROE JR.

These questions were not for the sake of curiosity alone. For some reason, in that brief passing moment, their lives became relevant to me, and I genuinely became interested in their stories, but I had no clue as to why. Fortunately and unfortunately, there were plenty of people out in the world who were willing to put my curiosity to use.

The first place that this curiosity was used was in my local church. Ministry required that I go out into my community, meet people, pray for their needs, and offer an introduction into salvation. It was challenging, but I had a gift for making connections. The second place I experienced the intentional use of this curiosity was my time spent as a network marketer. Network marketing is nothing more than selling a product that for one reason or another you are passionate about. This is where I began to identify my curiosity as more of a symptom to my greater passion. I learned that I genuinely wanted to help people, and in order to do so, I had to know who they were. But before I would ever be able to help them, I first had to know who I was.

When we are young our minds are most vulnerable to outside influences. From an early age we are groomed to adopt the mindset that in order for our passion to thrive, it must be married to our careers. How many remember the question "What do you want to be when you grow up?" That question was often followed by "What do you like to do?" It is no wonder during career projects, I always gravitated to professions that helped people: doctors, lawyers, police officers, and such. I thought that the only way I would be able to help people is if I found my way into these fields. This fallacy could not have been further from the truth. Our passion is not committed to what we do, but rather who we are.

Since we carry ourselves with us everywhere, our identity is the optimal vehicle for our passion to travel in. It took a lot of combing through the weeds before I finally realized that my passion was designed to fit Billy. Not super Billy, mythical Billy, not the Billy that others wanted me to be, or famous Billy, just the compassionate, thoughtful, and caring Billy who simply wanted to make a difference in the lives of those he came across. Your passion is the same.

We can spend a lifetime feeling as if who we are is inadequate and never embrace our passion. However if we shift our focus from what we don't have to what we have to offer, we will learn that we are more than enough and our passion only needs 3 essential elements to thrive.

The 3 Essential Elements of Passion

Think of our passion as a flower in a garden. In order for the flower to grow it needs light, soil, water, and space. Without these components, the flower will more than likely die long before it grows to a full bloom. Like the flower, our passion has 3 essential elements that we must provide in order for it to thrive: exposure, nurture, and engagement. By providing these elements we keep our passion from losing momentum or overwhelming us as we support it.

Exposure

The first element, exposure, is important because a hidden passion can never impact the world. What is the point of being a passionate architect if you never design a building? Exposure assures us that our passion will be experienced by others by taking our passion out of the hidden environment of theory and bringing it into the light of the real world. This helps us better align our understanding of our passion with how we share our vision for it with others.

On the other side of exposure, presentation begets preparation. Knowing that our passion is going to be exposed creates accountability around it and the other 2 essential elements it is reliant upon. If you know you have guests coming over to your house, do you not straighten it up before they arrive? When we know something is going to be seen, we attempt to make it presentable. Our passion is no different. By removing surprise from the equation of our passion, we are able to embrace the knowledge that its exposure is inevitable and ensure that we are not caught unprepared. Remember your proactive approach and stay at the ready.

Nurture

The second element, nurture, speaks directly to our passion's desire for growth and expansion. If we want to expand our passion's influence we have to become intentional about how we are going to enrich it. The fact is, a malnourished passion lacks the substance necessary to create sustainable change in us, let alone enact change in others. As I stated in the beginning of the book, at no point am I going to ask you to quit your job. However, whether you decide to use your passion as the financial means to fund your lifestyle or not, I am going to ask that you strive to execute your passion at a level that is worthy of compensation.

I often receive a visceral reaction from people when I talk to them about getting paid for their passion. Heck, I even see this reaction when I talk to myself about my own passions. But let me be very clear. EVERY passion has a level at which it can be monetized. The process to arrive there however, is not instantaneous. If you recall from chapter 4, in order to lead someone, you simply have to be ahead of their process. Though the thought of having a passion that we are compensated for can create immense pressure, the secret is that we receive compensation for our passion from the very beginning.

One of my brothers has always had a passion for dance. Over the past 2 decades I have had the privilege of watching his passion grow from a teenager practicing breakdancing moves on a piece of linoleum in the garage, to the owner of a dance studio. He nurtured this outcome by spending years attempting to understand not only the fundamental movements of dance, but more importantly the process of teaching those fundamental movements to others. Long before he had paying students, he garnered experience as an instructor by teaching his friends for free. Also, before he had an official studio, he was teaching students in the living room of his duplex. We may not realize it, but our initial compensation for our passion comes in the form of knowledge rather than currency. Eventually, if we earn enough knowledge, that knowledge can be converted into currency if we choose to do so. Though we are responsible for ingesting the information, the nurture process is not a task that we complete alone. The other crucial element of nurture extends to the people we allow around us as well.

My youth minister would always say, "What goes in you, will come out of you, and affect the world around you." Nurturing our passion is just as much about the people we keep in our inner circle as it is about the information that we ingest. When we have the wrong people around us, energy that we could spend on nurturing our passion is consumed by the distractions of either ignoring negativity or recovering from the drain that these people can produce. It is impossible for a person who is jealous and envious about our passion to be capable of genuinely supporting our pursuit to nurture it. To make our passion monetarily viable, we must cultivate relationships that are going to encourage us to stay engaged with our passion as we continue to acquire the necessary components to build upon it. Remember, any relationship is something that we can choose to either continue to foster or decide to discontinue at any time. We are never stuck. Our supporters don't always have to agree with us, but they do always have to come from a space of wanting to see our passion flourish.

Timeout: Embrace or Exile?

*Grab your **Passion Journal**. What type of people do you have in your tribe? Are those the people that will push you towards or chase you away from your passion? It is possible that we may like a person who is out of alignment with our long-term passion. If they are unwilling to come into alignment with our passion, as hurtful as it might be temporarily, we will have to choose what level of engagement we are going to allow them in our lives, if any at all.*

Evaluate up to the top 10 people in your tribe and determine if they elevate your passion or take away from it. Write the top 3 attributes that each one brings into your life. If the attribute adds to the elevation of your passion, take a moment to express your appreciation for their support. If the attribute takes away from your passion, commit to having the diffi-

BILLY F. WROE JR.

cult conversation about how they are out of alignment with your passion and decide if they are willing to become aligned. If they are not, you must make the decision as to how the relationship will proceed.

I understand how hard this exercise can be for you to complete, as I have had to have these conversations throughout the years with family members and current/former friends. I want to encourage you, that as challenging as these conversations can be, I have always come out on the other side of them better for it. The results were that I either removed opposition to my vision or gained deeper allyship with those closest to me. Whatever the outcome was, it truly turns out to be a win for both sides.

Engagement

Engagement is often the determining factor of whether our passion's impact experiences a failure to launch. Sitting idly waiting for luck to ignite our passion is like waiting for an Uber to pick us up without ever being requested. Can it happen, yes, but the odds are heavily stacked against us that it will not. When it comes to engaging with passion my motto mirrors that of Nike, "Just do it!" By engaging with our passion we provide a space for it to enter into our lives in a tangible way. In this space we learn how committed we are to interacting with it. Is our passion something that we will cease to engage with the moment we are embarrassed or things get uncomfortable? Better yet, will we compromise our passion's impact by allowing it to be corrupted in a manner that abuses the purpose of its original design? Without engagement, the answers to these questions are best guesses.

It is easy to say what you would do or would have done in a situation that you have never been in. However, once you are in the actual situation, you might find that who you thought you would be in it does not match your actions. Engaging with our passion presents us with the opportunity to know with certainty what our capabilities are by example, not by speculation. This knowledge empowers us to further pursue our passions. Even if we try and fail, we at least learn that we actually have what it takes to start in the first place. Be willing to engage with your passion as often as you can, so that you can learn the answers to some of those lingering what-if scenarios that keep you up at night.

These 3 essential elements to our passion keep our passion in the ideal environment for sustainable growth. Each time we feel that our passion reaches a plateau, it is important to check in with each element to ensure that they are functioning as intended. If we find that we are lacking exposure, nurture, or engagement, we should immediately commit to implementing an action that can jump start the missing element. The fortunate thing is the more we allow our passion to interact with these elements, the more natural passion will feel in our day-to-day life.

In short, by hiring our passion, we are choosing to hire the portion of ourselves that we desire to share with the world. When we embrace all that we have to offer in this space, we tap into the full potential of just how powerful of a force our passion can be. As easy as it can be to get lost in the scale of our impact, always remember that your passion is uniquely assigned to you. Don't be afraid to seek an opportunity for growth in every experience. If people grow tired of hearing about your passion, let that be their problem, not yours. Lastly, the most important thing of all, never forget that even if you don't have all of the tools today, who you are is more than enough to live the passion-driven life that we all desire.

What's Next? (How to Use the Book Going Forward)

Have you ever watched a movie multiple times and noticed new things each time you watched it? Maybe you realized that something was missing in a scene, or an intelligent detail in the background that you didn't notice the first couple times around. *Fire Your Job, Hire Your Passion* was never intended to be the one stop shop as to how your passion would be defined. I intentionally designed it to be a foundation to which your own unique experiences of pursuing your passion could be built upon. That being said, I encourage you to make this book yours, by treating it as you would an old friend. You may not talk all the time, but when you do, you reminisce about old times, share new experiences, and learn new lessons from one another. From time to time, revisit your notes and the exercises that you found most impactful throughout this journey. If there is something that you want to add to the book add it. If there is something new that you obtain due to a new perspective, capture it. Your journey is 100% customizable to you.

As you continue to gain new experiences, allow the book to evolve with you. My hope is that the next time someone asks you "What do you do for a living?" you share with them your passion and not your profession. Not simply because it is what is currently trending in your mind, but because each day, no matter how you make a living financially, your passion inspires you to live a life rooted in connection. You just might be surprised at what they share with you in return.

It is my sincerest hope that all you have read in this book was uplifting and put you in a better position to pursue your passion like never before. I cannot begin to articulate how much sharing this project with you has meant to me, but I am thankful for the immense feelings of appreciation and gratitude that I have for your dedication to keeping your commitment to make this journey with me. They say that the greatest form of love is a sustained change of actions. I challenge you to take all that you have learned during this time, about yourself, your habits, your passions, your shortcomings, and even your community, and with it become the greatest love story that your passion has ever known. Congratulations on completing *Fire Your Job, Hire Your Passion*!

About the Author

A native out of Sacramento, CA, with over 25 years of experience in retail, recruiting, sales, management, and analytics, Author Billy F. Wroe Jr. has a diverse professional background. As an inspirational speaker and empowerment coach, he has worked with individuals, groups, and companies to help optimize productivity in leadership communication. Over the years, Billy has adopted the leadership concepts inspired by Stephen Covey, John Maxwell, Brian Tracy, Les Brown, and a host of other phenomenal inspirational speakers. His advanced comprehension of emotional intelligence has guided him in creating content that resonates with the heart of the human experience.

As a dedicated husband, father of 4, and friend, Billy possesses a gift to connect deeply when building rapport. By identifying with his audience, not as an expert, but as a compassionate mentor, he embraces vulnerability when sharing both his faults and successes during interactions. Rather than telling people what they need to do to achieve their goals, he focuses on guiding them to discover solutions for themselves.

Credits (Dedications)

God the Original Creator

- To the Most High, thank you for trusting and allowing me to make it through all of these life experiences to complete this work. I know that it could not have been me alone to bring this book into the light. You are the ultimate example of servant leadership. I pray that these words reach the hearts of the very people you designed them to touch.

My Love - Chasity

- You had to put up with a lot during the creation of this book. Sometimes I snapped at you while you were giving me feedback. Other times you would roll over in bed to find that I had been typing in the office for hours. Thank you for your support throughout this journey and I look forward to seeing how this work will add to our future and the future of our children.

<u>My Sisters</u>

- Jenn
  - The best friend that I could ever ask for. You have always made room for me at your table. Thank you for your listening ear and deep-cutting advice throughout the years. Your unwavering faith in me has pulled me out of some of my lowest moments. I hope that you see

this book as a memoir of the many milestones of our friendship.

- JC
  - Jenn number 2. Who knew I needed 2 Jenns? Not only have we had so many deep conversations that were the inspiration for this journey, you never stopped asking me when my book was coming out. I mean never. Thank you for believing in me and valuing me in such a way that I was able to trust the information that I gleaned throughout the process.

- Taralyn
  - When I say accountability partner it is an understatement. When you have someone who is willing to read over 150 pages of your work in its rawest form, that is not something that you come across everyday. From the day we met virtually, to the present, we have always had a connection. Thank you for your sisterhood, partnership, and mentorship. Most of all, thank you for your friendship.

My Brothers

- Shawn
  - Afro Can. Brother you have never doubted your little brother's ability to bring light to this world. As an author, you have shown me that we are capable of creating literary works beyond social media posts. Thank you for encouraging me to join the author ranks.

- Trenton
  - You have read tons of my smaller works, so it only felt right to give you something with more substance to add to the list. I highly value our friendship and your opin-

ion on the many world topics that we have discussed throughout the years. You don't find many people in the world that grow and stay consistent at the same time. I hope this book gives us more conversation topics to talk about throughout the years.

- Anthony
  - We always have conversations about manhood and our responsibility to protect our investment. This book is a testament to our brotherhood. Through tears of joy and tears of pain, being able to knock on your window as an adolescent whenever I was struggling with issues kept me from falling into some dark places. It is but for the grace of God, and your compassion that I am alive and well today. For that, I am forever in your debt.

- Tim
  - Brother from another. You have been an outstanding confidant throughout the past 3 decades. Thank you for sharing your wisdom with me through many of the challenges that I have experienced during my journey. It is an honor to be the man that you would entrust to guide your son as his godfather. Continue to be the light in your family as you are a shining example to more than just your household.

- Key
  - You were the person who told me about *The Secret*. It was our initial book exchange that helped me understand how this type of book would be written. In addition, you have been an all-star of a brother, from helping me understand real estate, to being willing to engage in our weird deep conversations about everything. Continue to stay true to your identity. I hope to one day read a book of your creation, so I can provide

just as much support to you as you have to me over the years.

- R&B$_2$
  - Is the greatest! To Roger and Brandon, though we are all doing our own thing these days, I want you to know that you 2 will forever be my brothers. I am continually inspired as I watch you both relentlessly pursue your passions. Your growth throughout the years has been nothing short of amazing. I hope that my passion for writing adds another notch in the belt of our shared accomplishments. I love you both.

- Point
  - To Michael, it is easy to come into someone's life when things are good, but not often does a person sign up for a complete catastrophe. When I was hurting so bad that I was on the verge of ending my life you stepped up to the plate. Thank you for being a brother no matter whether we lived in different states or down the street. This book is here today because when I was ready to give up, you wouldn't throw in the towel. I hope this book makes you proud.

- Bruce
  - While I was quietly building, you were vocally and financially supporting me. There are a lot of people that say let them know if you need anything, but you mean it with all sincerity. You often have told me that my content was a crucial catalyst to your growth, but know that your words and belief in me have been one of the driving forces for me to complete this book. Thank you.

My Parents

- Mom
  - Though I have always been an independent child, you have always been there. Your acceptance of my thoughts helped to give me the strength to share my voice with others. I hope that this book reflects favorably upon your efforts to raise an upstanding man, and more importantly, a father for your grandsons to model themselves after.

- Dad
  - Growing up you taught me about the importance of legacy. I could not introduce myself without hearing about your athletic ability. Though I did not follow your steps in the sense of athletics, I am carving my own legacy on a different path. Thank you for your unwavering belief in me, for allowing me to experience failure at a young age, and for showing me firsthand what work ethic looks like.

My Legacy

- Ezekiel
  - To my firstborn, the one who catapulted me into adulthood. Before you were born, I was unclear as to where I was heading in life. Your birth helped to clarify my purpose and passion for not only seeing the best in people but also the importance of helping them achieve it. As you continue your journey into adulthood, know that I am proud to be the father of such an amazing human. I love you Z.

- Elijah
  - To my second born, as silly as you can be, you often remind me of who I was as a child. I know I have been hard on you, but know that I come from a place of love. You are a phenomenal kid and almost every time I talk to a person who has met you, they have such wonderful things to say about you. We still have a little time left before you are a young man and out on your own, but I want to encourage you to hold on to the light that you shine. It is important to the world. I love you son.

- Ethan
  - To my third born, there is so much that I want for you in this world, and I want you to know that you can have it all. Though you may be too young to grasp this book right now, I hope that one day you read it and expand upon the legacy that I am leaving behind. I love you Manny.

- Nia
  - To my daughter, God knew that we needed each other. Thank you for embracing the relationship that I wanted to build with you as a father. I hope that as a father I am setting the standard of what love looks like from a man. Know you are now my legacy and with that comes all the love that you have always deserved. Sometimes in life it feels like we are being aimlessly developed, but when it comes to fatherhood, I know that God had you in mind when I was being designed. I love you and am so honored to be connected to you.

To my godchildren (Alexia, Samson, Noah, and Isabelle)

- As a godfather, I am the backup should something happen to your parents. I want you all to know that whether your parents are present or not is irrelevant to the support that I am willing to provide to you all. I hope that as you continue to grow, you all strive to achieve everything that you want out of life. Know that no matter how many times you fail, you can dust yourself off, try again and give it another shot. The sky's the limit.

<u>My Tribe</u>

- Everyone in my tribe, you all played a part in this book. There is not enough gratitude I could amass to thank you all. Watching you all live in your greatness and overcomer spirit has been an inspiration to keep myself going. This is our work, I just happen to be the current tribal representative. I hope this reflects well on us all.

Learn more about the 1stWroe at www.1stWroe.com

For booking details for Billy F. Wroe Jr, please email
bookings@1stWroe.com

Connect with us on: YouTube, IG, Facebook,
LinkedIn, & Twitter @1stWroe